DRAGONFLY IMAGO

DRAGONFLY IMAGO

Sailing the Dream: A Personal Journey

Patricia Gogay

Book Guild Publishing
Sussex, England

First published in Great Britain in 2011 by
The Book Guild Ltd
Pavilion View
19 New Road
Brighton, BN1 1UF

Typesetting in Garamond by
Keyboard Services, Luton, Bedfordshire

Printed in Great Britain by
CPI Antony Rowe

A catalogue record for this book is available from
The British Library

ISBN 978 1 84624 556 5

For Ken

Many a man's dream has floundered because of a woman, and many a woman's dream has faded because of a man. I now believe that for the same reasons dreams can also flourish.

'What the caterpillar calls the end of the world, the master calls a butterfly.'
Richard Bach, *Illusions*

Imago

Whether fly, moth, butterfly or beetle, insects live two lives. On land, the egg hatches into a grub or caterpillar. In that first lifetime they eat voraciously – perhaps they learn things too. The destiny of most is to become food, others are just unlucky numbers and fail to beat the odds.

If laid in water, the egg hatches into a nymphal form, which for those that survive guarantees a more generous allocation of life time – a full two years may pass before it crawls out onto land to begin a second existence. They also eat voraciously – perhaps *they* learn things too.

And then one day, halfway up a stem, in mid leaf even, an evolutionary bell rings out: that's it, time up, last call!

Ordinary maggots secrete a substance, which hardens around them. Upmarket maggots wrap their previous life in silk, though it can hardly matter whether they take their final rest in a fibrous overcoat or a grand sarcophagus since, as far as they can know, they are dead.

Inside the cocoon, the incredible process of metamorphosis takes place. Oblivious to any charge that there has been a deception, the cells reorganise themselves, change their names, a *this* becomes a *that*. The evolutionary bell rings out once more, the graves split open to release their second self, their final form – an imago.

Imagine adding those two uncommon denominators: free will and consciousness – learning things would then be much more likely.

Contents

Introduction

A walnut craft with a matchstick mast: or simply a leaf that has curled around its edges. See there, on the bankside, a fat-limbed toddler urges her frail ship onwards – she and it will share at least a million adventures.

Leaping from tussock to tussock as if they were mountain tops, she keeps pace with her boat. She watches intently as it crashes into iceberg pebbles, is becalmed in seaweed moss, almost lost in a gale force breeze. Excited, waving, she can still see it, all is well. Finally the boat disappears around a bend in the river and in her imagination she travels with it.

Her anxiety is only calmed by that night's dreaming when the walnut craft, because she willed it so, meets with the open sea – its only proper fate.

A man and a woman meet in middle age. With a mutual caution that comes from old hurts, they begin a love affair. Each has brought to the relationship the usual quota: a few gifts, a disproportionate amount of emotional baggage. As the years go by, the gifts become more valuable, the baggage is absorbed or relabelled and sent to a different destination. Some of it stays but it doesn't seem to matter much any more.

Side by side, working together, they build a boat and sail it around the globe only to find that they had discovered the treasure long before they set sail to seek it.

And for the woman, a long ago memory of a walnut craft became an allegory, a happy ending to what is politely called a troubled life.

Book One

The Caterpillar Years

'You need to describe something of who you are,' said my friend, 'your relationship to the rest of the world. People will be interested in such a drastic change of lifestyle.'

I protested, felt panicked, remnants of fear surfaced, which first surprised then disappointed me.

'It will distract from the story,' I tried, 'it's not the emphasis I want, this is about Ken, not me.'

My friend insisted. 'But you did it together and it is you, after all, who is telling about it.'

So I sat down to remember, looked for the relevance, recognised once again the patterns that had emerged from what some would describe as a troubled life.

But a drastic change in lifestyle? Perhaps not.

Throughout the horrors of the Second World War, indeed perhaps to spite them, babies were still being born, as I was, in Birmingham, England, in 1942. And now and again, as I was, abandoned a few weeks later at the offices of the local authority. Soon afterwards I was evacuated to an orphanage in Wales, a place called Garth that lies somewhere in the Conway Valley.

It was there in 1946 that I met one of those significant people who enter into every life, who may or may not be angels or even know that they are so. They can change a life through their connection with you, sometimes with only a word of encouragement or the offer of a new perspective. They are not usually forceful people but they are invariably kind.

My first such angel took form in a young teacher called Peggy Smith. She had a gifted, intuitive way with children who, because of it, adored her. She was pretty, too, though children do not know about that since pretty to a child is a smiling mouth and bright eyes and a face that will come close to yours.

The scar and the fringe that hides it are still there on my forehead from when I tobogganed into instead of around a Welsh boulder. Miss Peggy was third into focus after the revolving universe and the blackness.

'Look,' she said, pointing, 'look at the pretty red drops in the snow!' I looked, they were pretty. So I did not cry until they were putting in the stitches. As I say, she was gifted. In a photo from that time, a group of small children are gathered around the pond in the garden of the orphanage. Miss Peggy has a newly born lamb in her arms. I am sitting closest to her, wrapped up warmly in winter coat and mittens. Fair, naturally wavy hair, a shy, tight-lipped smile, small features in a tiny face. A pretty little girl child.

Miss Peggy really liked me. She sometimes took me to her parents' home for weekends and holidays. Even then I can remember what a special, picked out from the crowd feeling that gave me. It was fairy godmothers, sparkling wands, and magic. Getting ready to go was wonderful, my hands would be clasped together tightly or patting my sides, because if you didn't hang on tight you would burst with excitement. Peggy's parents lived in Birmingham. We travelled there by train. How I loved trains, the clattering rhythm of them, the going somewhere, the whole world passing by the window. When the carriage was full Peggy would have me on her lap. No one else did that. It felt warm like sun does, cocooned, loved.

Mr and Mrs Smith had a pond in the garden like the one at the orphanage but also a piano in the 'best' room. There were pictures on the walls, mostly of birds painted by Vernon Ward and Peter Scott. The house was situated at the end of a long cul-de-sac so Mr Smith had a good half acre of land. Most of it was taken up by parking and lock-up garages for trucks and cars but the area around the house was where he kept his 'dig for victory' vegetable garden, his chickens, pigs, a bad-tempered cockerel, two dogs, and best of all, a cat that they said was mine. Having a small business like that as well as a proper job at a radiator company placed the Smith family somewhere in the lower middle of middle class. The fact that he did not drink may well have added another point or two.

'If you really loved me you would adopt me.'

Peggy's mother cried when I said that. I don't know whether they had even thought about it but they must have contacted the Department of Social Services soon afterwards or there would not have been that fateful day at the court.

I was five and a half years old and it had been a terrible mistake to utter that wish.

The hearing was long and protracted. I was parked in the waiting area next to the courtroom, then ignored. No sunlight, nothing to eat or drink, not a book to look at, nor even a picture on the green and yellow walls. The oilskin covering of the bench seats had worn through to the backing, in places it had been slashed. Stuffing leaked out like layers of bracket fungi; it had the same fusty smell as the damp dead wood on which it might have grown. Even for a patient child, the passing hours became intolerable. I resorted to picking off pinchfuls of the stuffing, spitting on it, rolling it into pellets wet enough to stick to the walls when I threw them.

Inside the courtroom, behind the heavy soundproof doors, a catastrophic decision was being made.

Before an adoption application was heard, rigorous enquiries had to be made about the child's origins and whether there might be living relatives. Somehow, even though I was officially registered as an orphan, my birth mother had been located and contact made. Behind that heavy panelled door, while I made pellets from the stuffing of the benches, she was screaming, beseeching the court to give her back her child. I suppose the judge tapped his gavel on his desk at the close of the proceedings; he might just as well have donned the black cap before solemnly telling me about the place of execution.

There were no farewells with the Smiths – perhaps they were upset. Instead, I was carried from the waiting-room and into the street on the shoulders of a strange man. The weather was appropriate: a dark violet winter afternoon, drizzling with rain. Every street and vehicle light looked as dizzy as I felt. They swayed with the rhythm of the man's walking. Having never been carried aloft like that before, I was so terrified of falling, made so tense and catatonic by it that I could not cry.

A year and two days it lasted – sometimes I think I can remember each one of them. My mother (and the man) lived in a dilapidated terraced house at 42 Moseley Road. I think there was a rent book. Two rooms downstairs with an add-on scullery, two up and the attic room, which would be mine just to sleep in since the only furniture in it was a bed. Outside, a walled tarmac garden led out to an entry way that served the back of the houses. All the homes in the row looked exactly alike, flat fronts and sash windows like a mouthful of perfectly capped but nicotine-stained teeth. The bomb that destroyed the house next door had been surgical in its precision. The gap in the middle stood out like a missing incisor. The row of houses leered out at the world. The acrid smell from burned timbers joined with cabbage, onions and damp laundry, giving an identity to the inside of our house that was both permanent and personal. It was a drab, squalid shelter. Pinched, ugly and loveless. Within a week I contracted scabies.

There were two other children in the house: Fred and Rita; both younger than I. Strange to remember their names still when I cannot recall the name of my mother or even her face. The only part of her I can see is the printed headscarf she wore with its black and white terriers.

Poverty was a post-war fact of life, common enough at that time to be irrelevant except for the most privileged, but there were fewer of them in those days. It carried no sense of deprivation then or now, whatever today's smug politicians might say about their triumph over slum origins. Food is food, no matter that the jam or condensed milk was put to unbuttered bread or that beef dripping was a feast. No, it was 'being sent' that embarrassed me so.

'I'm going to send you,' she would say, my mother.

So I would be pushed out into the street, over the Cardinal

Red step. Those bloody doorsteps! Such a vanity they were. No matter how modest one's station in life – the hand-me-down clothes, shoes that did not fit – it was vulgar, or common (which was even worse than vulgar) not to have a polished front doorstep painted from a tin of Cardinal Red every few days. A neglected front doorstep? That everyone could notice? Never! You could see the women doing it, stooped or kneeling in headscarves, bibbed pinafores, even in curlers and housecoats sometimes. I am ashamed of what I felt then because I realise now that it was about staying 'respectable', not giving in. A show of resistance against the war, a very feminine way of dealing with it. There was defiance in the gesture, braveness also.

'I'm going to send you,' she would say.

To the butcher for 'something to boil', just another week of credit please; round to the back of the market stalls in the centre of Birmingham, which was known then as the Bull Ring, to collect up leaves and trimmings from cabbage and cauliflower; to a neighbour for that now infamous music-hall joke: the cup of sugar. The five Woodbines, the accumulator for the wireless.

My mother rented the back room to a lodger. A usual enough arrangement in those days of housing shortage and making do. Chris seemed old to me but may not have been. He always looked grizzled because of the trembling which made shaving difficult; I think my mother did it for him sometimes. Now I realise he had Parkinson's disease.

His skin was horrible: scaly and shedding, especially on his feet. Trapped and unlovely, Chris spent his long, solitary hours fiddling with small pendulum clocks, making them chime again, polishing the casings, oiling the moving bits. Every Friday he would struggle into shoes, something it took an hour for him to do. One of us would tie the laces.

Three doors down on the left, at the butcher's shop, he would buy an odd cut of meat that was rolled and stuffed – mother said it was skirt of lamb. He would boil this on the open coal fire in his room; made it last the week.

I became both helper and companion to Chris. His speech was unintelligible – hoarse, slurred noises – but I came to understand his out-of-control hands and gestures, helped him clean the clock parts, shared his pleasure when they chimed again, pulled his curtains morning and evening, cut up the meat on his plate.

Early in the evening he would sit on the edge of his bed and I would lift and swing those awful-looking feet so that he swivelled onto the mattress; often enough to genuinely not mind that the flakes of skin had to be brushed off my pinny.

Sometimes he fell down and could not get up again; then I would have to call my mother to help him. If he fell in the night he would stay trapped between the bed and the chest of drawers until morning when I would find him. I cried bitterly every time I found him like that and never mentioned that his trousers were sometimes wet.

Returning through the back gate of the yard one day, after shopping with my mother, I heard a terrible wailing sound, high notes that seagulls make. My mother guessed. Dropped the shopping. Ran to the house. When I got there she was in the back room. As I put my head around the door she shouted.

'Get out!'

But I had seen and I knew. She had wrapped a tea cloth around his head but you could smell it – the hair, the burning.

Chris had fallen from his chair. It was where he always sat, close to the open fire. His head had fallen onto the burning coals, he could not get away. He died at the hospital two days later. How often I have wondered since, did they have morphine then? Please, did they have morphine?

Perhaps it was to console me that I was given the kitten to care for. A tiny black one, barely able yet to focus its eyes. It was kept in a wire cage, outside in the yard because my mother did not like them but I was allowed to let it out to play with me several times a day. I loved its furry warmth, the way it would box at my fingers with its tiny paws. I fed it with slices of bread, lettuce leaves and potato peelings. One morning it was missing from its cage even though the bent nail holding the door closed was still in place. Nobody would tell me anything about it. My mother shrugged. They let me look for it – it seemed days and days that I looked for it.

It was then, I think, that an already bleak and rarely warming sun simply vanished from my sky. A desolation took its place, a bad seed was planted, a rage was born. The truth, of course, is that the kitten probably died from starvation.

By then I was wetting the bed most nights, which sent my careworn mother into rages. These sometimes ended in violent spankings. I remember the time she carried me by scruff and knickers into the yard then threw me up into the air. She was running out of patience.

She packed a suitcase for me once.

'I want to go back to Mrs Smith.'

'Right!' she said, biting down on the word before she let it out. She packed a small suitcase furiously, pushed me out over the Cardinal Red step, kept pushing. Every few yards she pushed me. I felt hope surge through me, strong as the kick from adrenaline; soon we would be at the bus stop. Then she began to yell, grabbed the case, pushed at me all the way back.

Yet finally it was the grey army blanket that ended it all. As if it were in front of me now, I can see the heavy woollen stitching around its edges, feel the rough, sack-like texture, smell its particular animal odour. Laid out on the floor in the cramped space between the table and the cooking range, the two items that took up most of the space in the living-room. The man who had carried me from the court house was lying there with me. He did not have any clothes on. He was rubbing part of his body between my thighs, nudging and rocking at me. I don't know how long it went on. I knew it wasn't right. I noticed the wet patch on the blanket when he set me on the table to dress me. He would get into terrible trouble if he, too, had wet the bed.

Embarrassed, powerless, a helpless little grub. An extraordinary mix of emotions, some of which belong in a child, others so adult that they may even be innate. And I remember them. Asking him to stop. 'I don't like it, daddy.' Fury when he totally ignored me. Then fear at being so powerless. A grown woman in me somewhere, praying that my mother would not walk in suddenly, see whatever wrong thing this was and blame me: that was a terrible and frightening thought. They were the same feelings I had when he washed us. I dreaded my mother giving him that task when she was too busy to do it. He would wash the younger ones first because they both fitted in the portable zinc bath. He would insist on me standing up in the bath and he took much longer washing me: sometimes the water got cold before he finished. My mother always used a flannel but he used his hands, soaping and stroking just with his hands, over and over. Six years old and embarrassed. Sexually embarrassed. Knowing nothing at all about 'something'. It was cruel.

I am uncertain as to how soon afterwards it was, in relation to these events, but the skipping rope was looped several times around my neck, crossed over the wooden handles so that it did not slip. My sister Rita had the long end.

'Pull it,' I said to her.

Too young to see more than a joke, she pulled with all her might, toppling over backwards, shoes erupting the gravel where she slid as she tugged, squealing with glee. Even so, young as she was, pulling with all of her weight was enough: the neck was small, the noose tightened, my knees buckled.

Too much noise going on. My mother wondered about it, glanced through the scullery window, then she screamed.

A telephone call from the nearest kiosk.

'I can't have her, she's affecting the other children.'

Both Peggy and Mr Smith had come to the house sometimes to take me for excursions in the car or for a cake and sandwich tea at a Lyons Corner House. If Mrs Smith came with them she always stayed in the car. I think the reception was cool but Peggy would become a headmistress before she was 30 and even then she was not easily deterred. They had noticed the growing vagueness in my eyes, the bruising, the general symptoms of abuse. Peggy was especially appalled to learn that when the authorities came to take me to hospital they found maggots breeding in my saturated bed.

Yet they will not know, unless they come to read this ultimately happy story, anything about Chris, the kitten or the grey army blanket. I didn't tell because kids don't; they experience things and the feelings that go with them but cannot construct the story or its meanings. And so they all remained my own dark secrets until I was 20 years old. Not that I deliberately hid them, just that it served no useful purpose to talk about it. I mean, who would want to know about such things, and why?

It was felt prudent to keep me in hospital for a time. There must have been some concern about such a young child making a suicide bid even if it was only a gesture that went wrong. Afterwards I again lived in various children's homes. Barnardo's was fine: pocket money, outings, expectations of nice behaviour such as eating properly with a knife and fork then laying them side by side on the plate. There was a rocking horse in the games room; you were even allowed to soak cartoon transfers in saucers of water and press them onto the back of your hand. Erdington Cottage Homes was awful. I doubt if there truly was a huge cauldron boiling on the Aga range at the far end of the dining-room or a fierce fat cook presiding over it at mealtimes but I do remember how Dickensian it all seemed. The cook made us all so fearful that we decided she was a genuine witch who might even boil a naughty child in her cauldron.

Gradually the pattern of weekends and holidays with the Smith family was re-established. The wish and whisper of every orphan child held promise again: to become the heroine of the fairy-tale, live in a real family.

Another photo, again taken beside a pond because it was the prettiest spot in the Smith garden. Me in a summer frock, a ribbon in my hair, Peggy's younger sister Brenda standing behind, both hands resting affectionately on my shoulders. Another with Peggy herself. She is wearing a smart linen suit and a hat. My new family were not ones for taking photographs so it was nice to think that they, too, found this occasion a special moment to record.

We had all anticipated that day in a mood of confidence and pleasure. It was a putting right of things. Today I shall be officially adopted and live with them for ever. After the hearing, we would all go to Lyons Corner House for a full high tea. For me and me alone there would be a Knickerbocker Glory, which in those days was the ultimate ice-cream sundae. Chocolate, vanilla and strawberry with a delicious mortar of red syrup between, topped with cream, crushed nuts and its final flourish, a single glistening glacé cherry. I had planned a solemn thank you gesture, I would give the crowning cherry to Mrs Smith – my mother. There was such a sense of goodness and virtue in that idea of sacrifice that I practised the doing of it, savouring the emotion with the self-satisfaction and solemnity of an eleven-year-old. Mrs Smith would give it back to me of course!

But I was never to play out that carefully rehearsed gesture. There was the tea, the Knickerbocker Glory too, but everyone was so subdued as if only indulging me because they had promised. They had suspended talk, exchanging glances that were nonplussed and disbelieving. Mother did not eat her macaroon, her favourite. But I heard the remark from Mr Smith. How stylish he had looked that day in a tweed jacket over a waistcoat that showed his pocket watch chain. A Pickwickian man, balding, stout, upright. He shook his head.

'They weren't going to, were they missus?' Mother shushed him. Years later she would tell me that my birth mother had created a dreadful scene again, 'carried on alarming', as they say in the Midlands.

'I'm married now,' she had told them, 'the house is decorated, regular income, all my other children are with me.' Turning to accuse Mrs Smith, she shouted at her, 'You have no right to steal my child.' Appalled, Mrs Smith had flinched at that, then cried. At that point the judge called for a recess during which the families were separated. A potential for violence had developed from what everyone had expected to be a short, formal procedure leading to a happy outcome.

After the recess the judge cleared the courtroom of all but the social services people, the clerk and the usher before calling me in to sit with him at the table below the rostrum.

'You are rather a special little girl,' he said. 'I'm told that you are usually top of the class at school, that you are very well behaved. We all want you to have a good life, Patricia, and to be happy. Your mummy says that she wants you to be with her now, what do you think about that?'

I wonder about it sometimes: what it was that made up his mind. Whether he was wise enough, knowing enough, to look at my face, its expression; whether he understood why I spoke so quietly, in such a choked back whisper so that he had to ask me to say it again.

'I would rather go back into the homes than live with my mother.'

I was not present when the decision was made so I did not hear his reasons but I knew from the way Mrs Smith held me and I knew from the way Mr Smith walked off a little way, fumbling for his handkerchief, that I was theirs now. Official, proper, permanent, safe.

And I never saw my real mother again...

Book Two

The Chrysalis Years

There is a latent period in childhood, a generous spacing that separates the wow and astonishment of infancy from the later turbulence of youth. These chrysalis years of consolidation and becoming are a particularly fine example, it seems to me, of one of nature's clever strategies. As we prepare for that next explosion of mental and physical energy, the one that will shape our future life, earliest memories are put on hold, some may disappear entirely, a few are put on stand-by.

Not long after the final adoption proceedings, what was left of the Smith family, which now included me, moved to an old gatekeeper's lodge just north of Worcester. Sister Brenda had married. Peggy had chosen to live in Germany, to become a headmistress and to follow the German prisoner-of-war with whom she had fallen in love.

Bevere Lodge is a place where you would want to leave your bones. The house itself was small and in disrepair but the setting was perfect. It stood alone at the end of a long avenue of oak, sycamore, and elm. The huge wrought-iron gates that once safeguarded the propriety of the manor house were still in place. The manor itself, built on the high ground overlooking the River Severn, was a mile or so further up the lane.

Most of the garden was a large copse, though nearly large enough to qualify as a small wood. It hid and harboured two spring-fed ponds, one of which was a ribbon of water, the other a smaller round pond: my favourite of the two, the most secret. This was the one with an island in the middle; a solitary tree grew there; barely two yards wide my island was.

These were my Mark Twain, Laurie Lee and Dylan Thomas years. Just as they had done I experienced it all with the eyes and the mind of a boy child. Yet in truth I was neither boy nor girl. My mother did not impose either her own or society's expectations with regard to sexual identity and I can tell you now that to be left to discover it for yourself is a glorious thing. I realise now that I have never ceased looking at the world that way.

Trees were practical, useful things from which could be fashioned bows and arrows, threshing sticks for jungle fantasies, fishing rods, dislodgers of hazel-nuts; initiable, burnable, climbable. Then one day, so suddenly as to make you gasp, they become inexplicably beautiful. The pocket knife is put away – eventually lost somewhere.

I hacked away the soft insides of a fallen tree. My canoe became a ship, took me to the island, hovered over the water lilies where the big solitary perch peered with concentrated eyes through a picket fence of stalks, poised and waiting for a kill. I fished for hours, so still, so patient, that water rats and voles took up their daily business around me. With no one else around who might lift their feet, or shudder, I saw nothing that was ever scary or ugly. A snake caught a frog. I watched curiously, without pity, the way the hinged jaws lay back against its eyes, its length convulsed, contorting over its meal.

I learned about the ways and habitats of all the fish. Rudd, tench, perch, chub, roach, loaches, miller's thumbs. I lay for hours on my belly, peering into the water, marvelling at a teeming universe that dived and crawled, skated and writhed.

Eels stretched upright among the lily stems, took up their same swaying rhythm. The boy child in me interfered, poking them with a stick just to let them know they couldn't fool me. Quick as a blink, they snapped back into their hole in the mud, raising a puff of sediment which set off a chain reaction among the others. When the mud settled all you could see, if you knew about it of course, were their sequin eyes, their pulsing throats.

I ruined spiders' webs and stickleback nests. Having a Zen approach towards calamity, showing no sign of fuss or belligerence, they simply did it all again.

They are far too many to describe, those thousand upon thousand small encounters. Birds, butterflies, mayfly hatchings, stag beetles, wasp nests, giant puffballs, violets and celandines – and still I look for them.

* * *

Mr Smith would only enjoy two years of his retirement before suffering and dying of stomach cancer. I was oddly unmoved by his death, only understanding later why that was. Mother and I were alone at Bevere now and I loved being with her. We split the winter supply of logs, properly, with full over-the-shoulder strokes, tended the garden, shopped in Worcester once a week, made the two mile walk to the bus stop a pleasure together. I culled the kittens, doing it the same way I had seen Mr Smith do it: a hard no-nonsense blow to the head against the dustbin lid to concuss them before holding them down in a bucket of water to drown.

I'm no longer acquainted with that person who could extinguish a warm, nuzzling, mewling life with such clinical detachment. Yet the only difference is that of compassion. I could still dispatch a suffering animal but with sadness now – not indifference – not the work of a blind grub.

The passion I felt about wildlife in all its forms had this curiously detached aspect to it. I skinned and mounted a squirrel, a bird and a fish, which won the hobbies prize at school. One of the cats caught and killed a sparrow. I simmered it gently until the bones came free then reassembled them into a full skeleton, drilling and wiring the smallest of the bones. Wanting the structure to show up a startling white against the red mahogany of its case, I placed it carefully into a mixing bowl before covering it with concentrated bleach. An hour later the whole lot had dissolved into a chalky residue. My mother was astonished at my reaction to what was such a shame, such a calamity. I simply told her in the controlled voice of Spock in *Star Trek* that it should have been a five per cent dilution and that I should have monitored the effect more carefully. Then, like the sticklebacks and spiders I had watched as they repaired their ravaged nests, I did it all again.

Had she been trained in such insights, my mother might have been alarmed at such a controlled reaction. Whether good or bad I neither laughed nor cried. It was undoubtedly an early sign of the emotionless psychopathy that would eventually develop into a period of acute mental illness.

While I had overcome the bedwetting problem by the age of 14, I continued to bite my nails, especially when absorbed in a book. At 18 I was an intense, sombre adolescent. The memories that had been put on hold during these chrysalis years were beginning to resurface. The images were nasty, as if smirking and conspiring together, hiding behind trees, threatening to pounce, but I was 'never any trouble' as they say.

It may not happen any more but in my day when sixth formers left Worcester Grammar School for Girls they joined in a long tradition of throwing their boaters into the River Severn. It was usually done from the bridge close by the splendid cathedral that overlooks what must be one of the loveliest cricket grounds in England. The girls 'hurrahed'.

'Free,' they shouted, tossing boaters high into the air or skimming them across the water like discus throwers. Mine dropped limply through my fingers. I had loved everything about school, and now felt anything but free. The world beckoned with a crooked finger.

'Come, my pretty pretty,' it seemed to say in a voice that sounded sinister.

After so many schools and differences in curriculum, I was grateful enough to have several O levels and an A level in biology. I might have had a second, in divinity, was expected to, but no one noticed that I was ill or knew that I had deliberately spelled God without its Capital Letter as well as making it transparently clear that I was praying under false pretences.

Now I was almost 19. For the next 14 months I lived in the nurses' home at Worcester Royal Infirmary where I had enrolled to train as a State Registered Nurse. It was an extension of institutional life in many ways, except in having separate rooms to sleep in. Matron was deeply disappointed when I crept out of a window one night and refused to return. She telephoned me at home: I had gained top marks in the preliminary training school, had shown myself entirely suited to become a nurse, she just couldn't understand it.

'I'm so sorry, Matron,' I said. 'I cannot understand it either.'

I went home to Bevere. Peggy had returned from Germany to be with mother. As often happens with primary school teachers, she found communicating with an adolescent decidedly more demanding, and I was in no state to reward her for at least trying. Rather sad, really, since she had been my second mother. She was critical of her mother's handling of me. I think she had hoped that I would become gracious, charming, ladylike. What a disappointment! During the next few weeks the symptoms of depression, that blank anticlockwise spiral of misery, became impossible to disguise, nor was there any sign that it would simply pass, that I would 'grow out of it'. Not only was I unable to pull my socks up, I could barely bother to take them off at night.

Mother knew that I was contemplating suicide. I spent whole days alone by the side of the round pond. She would walk down that far to find me. It was something she had never done before so we both knew what that was about. It was the very thought that I might do such a terrible, ungrateful thing that became completely unbearable for me. She knew perfectly well how much I loved her. But it was only what I imagined I felt for her because at that time I had no idea of what love really was. The feelings I had for her were therefore entirely selfish. She was the teat I yearned for but had never suckled.

The breakdown finally arrived. Just walked through my door without knocking. Nothing hysterical or dramatic about it really but it stood there blocking the way.

'Hello, I'm here now so why don't you take a good long look at me instead of ignoring me when we pass in the street!'

It was like a forlorn attempt to swim to a shore that may or may not be that slightly thicker line on the horizon, then suddenly, with a sad resignation, letting yourself slip below the surface to drown. And, as in drowning, the mind contracts into a dense core of pure self in which state it can dissolve without regret. Another of nature's caring strategies: the way she prepares you for dying, the way she numbs the pain after a serious accident just in case it proves to be fatal. Nothing at all comes in from the outside world.

'I don't remember what happened,' says the victim.

Desperate to find me help, mother went into Worcester one day, determined not to return until someone could be made to understand that although her child was not threatening to burn down the house, had not attacked the milkman with an axe, or stamped on the toe of a policeman, she was nevertheless in urgent need of professional help.

The general practitioner said it would pass, the Church Man suggested she pray. Finally, late in the day, she found herself sitting in the office of an on-call social worker. I can see how mother would have appeared: an elderly woman, careful of her appearance in front of important people, hatted and gloved, sitting upright in her proud and gentle way. She would be tired by now, defeated, embarrassed at her temerity. And so when the kind-faced, middle-aged woman across from her leaned forward, touched her hand briefly, said, 'I hope I can help you, Mrs Smith,' my mother's own pent-up dam of compassion broke open and she wept.

To see an elderly person so deeply distraught is intensely sad and moving for anyone who cares though it is reasonable to wonder whether a male social worker would himself have been moved to tears as was this humane, rather beautiful person. Having someone weep with her was a freeing moment for mother: it spared her embarrassment, legitimised her concerns.

'She seemed so ordinary,' mother said to me later, by which she meant unpretentious. To hell with professional detachment!

An appointment was set up for me to be interviewed by a psychiatrist at the local psychiatric hospital in Powick village, which is situated several miles out of the city, in the rural flatland between Worcester and the Malvern Hills. A quilted landscape of pasture and cultivated fields. Cows and horses dotted here and there like stray stitches. Elgar country.

I don't know the history of the place but it was large, austere, period Victorian, in red brick, and having an indistinct character. Its size, together with a high separated position in the landscape, made it equally likely to be workhouse, prison or grand private house.

It was a strange, brief interview – suitably mad I suppose.

'Chris has come back ... he's different now, a ghost. I just see his white hands clutching the edges of the bed, by my feet. I cannot make out his face but he frightens me.'

Then I told the psychiatrist about the recurring dream.

'Every night it comes. I am looking out onto a lovely winter landscape. A full moon is slatted in two by the bough of a cedar tree. The snow is smooth, untouched. There is a profound stillness and I am breathing slowly, concentrating on the beauty of it all. Then, out of the corner of my eye, I see it coming, a huge, dark boulder. I dare not look. I hear it too: vibrations and thunder. Rolling down from a high place, it crashes in front of me then rolls over the land. When it has gone and I look out again everything is spoiled. I become a part of the desolation. Then I turn into a wolf and can hear myself howling at the moon.'

Next day I admitted myself into the hospital as a voluntary patient, which is what the psychiatrist had advised. Oddly enough it brought a feeling of relief. My sense of self, prepared as it was for drowning, was an amorphous, unconnected form. Some external structure might somehow prevent me disappearing altogether like left-over jelly down the sink.

Book Three

Metamorphosis

Together with several other women from the female ward, I was enrolled into a course of group therapy, a newish concept at that time. The psychiatric profession appeared to be engaged in a struggle to disengage from the passive, often lengthy, Freudian model of treatment in favour of more aggressive techniques. Electroconvulsive therapy (ECT), sleep therapy, abreaction, stupefying doses of sodium amytal, lithium, librium, lysergic acid dielthylamide (LSD). During the following eight months I was treated by all these means.

'You must let it all out, Pat.' So I did. It was like spitting out decomposing entrails. How shudderingly horrible to discover that such a rage had taken possession of me. Here was the dormant fire that burns in every belly, small as a pilot light with the potential of a furnace. Yet ultimately it would be healing, because the source is always fear.

Still the boulder crashed down from its high place. I fought it with a furious loathing; turned over hospital beds, regained consciousness after an ECT treatment to find my hands around the throat of a doctor. A nurse fractured her arm trying to calm me. I suppose I should feel grateful that they did not perform a lobotomy on me to separate the frontal lobes of my brain. Between one gladiatorial contest and the next I simply sat gazing at the floor and wept.

'Testing out,' they call it. You will prove yourself right, girl, sure you will, the world is indeed an impossibly hostile environment. Don't you have anything to do with it. If you push hard enough it will declare itself, lose patience, show you what it really is, admit the deception, confess that it is a deep mire-filled pit.

I am the four-year-old at the top of the stairs, stamping its foot, shouting, 'I hate you! I hate you! 'Yet all the while rigidly fearful of its bold, daring gamble. What if Mummy shouts back: 'I hate you too!'

Four-year-olds would never do it if, for even a moment, they imagined that might happen, because then you would be abandoned, left, alone. The pilot light would go out altogether. The Big Bad

Wolf, that elemental fear of aloneness, would eat you up – then belch.

Mental illness is healed, not cured. A cure suggests a neat surgical procedure in which the damaged tissue is excised, or a course of the appropriate antibiotic until you are symptom free. The psyche does not respond like that: you cannot excise experiences, they are written in indelible ink. They can only be re-evaluated, re-edited if you like, until one day you realise that when the snake eats the frog there is no malice in it, that it is not so much what has happened as how you perceived it.

Children lie about their past and that of course means that we all do. They don't do so with the intention to deceive but they hoard their grudges, hang on to slights and injustices until they have a decent collection, a nice swappable cupboard full, all in good condition for later trade-offs in the adult world.

My birth mother, while struggling with whatever had impoverished her spirit, had loved me just as much as she was able to. Now I remembered the days in the local park, the nights when she would leave the house with us when it was dark, walking until she found a bench to sit on. Then she would cry for what seemed a long time. When it stopped she would sigh over and over before finally rising up, like an old woman, to walk slowly back to the house in Moseley Road. All the selfish little child chooses to remember of such times is how cold and boring it was. What courage had it taken, I wondered, to beg a court to return me, to have to apologise for her circumstances, to suffer comparisons with a respectable and much more socially acceptable family, to not be wearing a hat.

How virtuous we think it is to forgive. What blame we issue when we do so. It would have been such a catharsis if I could have asked *her* to forgive *me*. Dealing with loss – of the family I had come to love, the kitten, Chris, sexual trust – wasn't nearly as difficult as dealing with shame.

Well I dumped all this complicated mess onto the psychiatrist and during the long process of re-editing my childhood memories she and I would become devoted friends. As well as being a rare and totally unexpected consequence and made of a substance that neither of us came to understand, she would remain my friend and mentor for a further 25 years until she died.

When at last I finally turned to look at the boulder, it was me, as it had been all along.

Fortunately the steps that must be taken before resuming a dialogue with the outside world were shallow and invalid friendly. Falteringly sometimes, a passion for life returned, would never again leave. Lose your life to find it? Liberate yourself from all those conventional excuses that we use to shield ourselves from the truth? Something like that.

Compared with far too many emotionally crippled youngsters life so far had only dealt me glancing blows. The sort of childhood I have described can spoil a life, of course, but to believe it inevitable, never to be offered a chance to re-edit the past, is to relinquish hope – something the human spirit will strenuously resist.

Setting out into the world again, as if for the first time, almost smiling now, I spent the next third of my life negotiating a compromise. Should I contain and discipline what was now an irrepressible compulsion to live, or find expression for it? Should I cast the boulder into the valley then follow it, or sit quietly, gratefully, beside it? The solution was easy – do both. Live with the compromise, but play with it, polarise it, make it lie somewhere between what is rational and what is impetuous. Eventually it would become a way of life and therefore no compromise at all.

It was a comfortable solution. I was still an introvert, still apparently unemotional, and very rarely laughed. Yet somewhere within me, closer to the surface than I could ever have thought possible, was a joy. Every day, whether bright or dull, this simmering happiness percolated away like coffee on a stove. In that frame of mind there was no ideology convincing enough to even suggest bartering today's experience in exchange for a supposedly better afterlife, inconceivable to imagine that anywhere else in the universe could be as beautiful. It was even possible to believe in the potential of human beings, however far it may lie in the future, to attain that love which 'passeth all understanding'.

Still, it was a restless compromise. I moved to London where I worked for six years in the pathology laboratory of a large hospital, then as a croupier for another six. Finally, when the time felt right, I attended full-time college as a mature student and became a probation officer. I wanted so much to be a person who would lean across, touch someone, and hope it would help.

The nightmare never did return but it lurked about somewhere so that as soon as life settled into a smooth rhythm, just when I felt competent and confident, I feared the boulder might descend again and spoil things. The past is never completely resolved, the gruesome history of the world is testimony to that, and a pre-emptive retreat was the only defence I could manage all by myself; besides, there was an excitement in changing route.

While I may have stayed in jobs for respectable periods of time, an obsessive restlessness was undeniable when it came to digs. My two suitcases and I must have shared over a dozen rented rooms all over London. As soon as a new key was set in my hand, cases on the bed, the ritual began: hairbrush here and just so, six books to line up, a few clothes to hang, two pictures for the walls. The same candlesticks, the same travelling clock, the same mug that was just the right size for toothbrush, paste and shampoo. Having personalised the room, stayed for a while to get the feel of it, I began looking for the next key – to another room.

I drove to Worcester three times a year to spend my holiday breaks with mother. Until she was 82 she would also come and stay with me. She was still strong but not so agile so I suppose it was a sensible decision for them to sell Bevere and move to somewhere more manageable. Logical, sensible – words I normally favoured – but this felt like a clock stopping suddenly, leaving an empty sound behind it. The house Peggy chose for them was suburban executive, characterless, one of a row in line, brand new. A tasteful, distinctive, refined accommodation – I loathed it.

In a scarcely deniable reaction to that event I next chose to live on a houseboat. The first was a small wooden cruiser that had served as one of the cheaper holiday hirings on the Norfolk Broads. I moved to Windsor where the boat was moored in a narrow cut off the main course of the River Thames. I nestled happily in its 24 feet of space, named it *Bevere*, returned to sharing life with swans, mallards, willow trees and fish. In the winter months the condensation from the ceiling dripped steadily onto the bed so I made a quilt of canvas because there was nothing that could spoil this certain feeling that I had finally come home. It is now 35 years since I lived in a house.

The second houseboat was the one I built. It was already a houseboat when I bought it but the superstructure was ruined and sodden with rot. After demolishing that completely I was able to salvage the steel pontoon on which it had been built. It, too, was only 24 feet long but its beam of twelve feet provided double the volume of the cruiser.

After it was hauled out I spent the next six months chipping and scraping off the rust before applying thick tar on top of red lead primer. How I did so is still a mystery to me, but I built a cottage style home complete with a sloping fibreglassed roof, and except for the multi-paned windows and the initial main framing I did it alone without a thought as to whether I could. When mother sold Bevere she had given me £500, which I thought of as a biblical talent that must be put to good use. I still felt guilty for the sorrow I had caused her and this created a very high level of motivation. I invested in the *Readers Digest* do-it-yourself book, which covered most aspects of the work but also found that I had remembered Mr Smith's tool shed with its spokeshaves, planes, electrical bits and plumb weights. The older men in the neighbourhood were more than happy to explain techniques and anticipate problems. The younger men wanted to take over and I wasn't too keen on the way they smiled about it all – patronising I think.

It was all wonderfully incongruous and perfectly fitted the compromise in its unrelenting energy, its hint of delinquency. During the day I lived in dungarees and wellies. By late afternoon I was spattered with paint, sawdust, tar, fibreglass. By 6pm, gilded, eyelashed, lipglossed, it was time to don the elegant uniform (a long skirt slit to the thigh) and drive into London to deal blackjack or spin the roulette wheel. A daily metamorphosis: drab cocoon to glittering wings; wellies to rhinestone sandals; grey sky to rainbows.

Though much preferring nests to barns, it was still a small area to live in. The bed had to be raised up into the false wall each morning to allow daytime walking space. I fancied eating at a dining-table, too. So, as middle age loomed, I began to look for a larger boat in which to accommodate the paraphernalia of a more settled lifestyle. What I once carried in two average-sized suitcases now necessitated a small van. The contents had not changed much, only the volume. Books and tapes, hobby materials, a pond-life aquarium, minimal clothes. The same tooth mug, the same pictures.

I settled on a 40-foot custom-built houseboat, this time moored on the main course of the River Thames, on the Wraysbury side, opposite the 'Bells of Ousley' pub, within rowing distance of that rather movingly understated pavilion, erected at Runnymede to commemorate the death of President Kennedy.

Here I was, 38 years old, a professional spinster, nice home, rewarding job, sexual relations now and again, which petered out of their own accord when it became clear that I would not marry or cohabit. Enough, sufficient, more than one might have expected. Settle now, be content, curb your enthusiasm – wear your corset! It was what I should do ... would try to do. I'd turn that record off, destroy it, never listen to it again. That breathless one from *West Side Story*. The one the young lover sings with such passionate optimism: something coming, something good, around the corner, maybe tonight...! Well at least I would try...

Book Four

Imago

Chapter 1

It was only a stray curl of a thought. One of those wisps and strands that will pass through a mind when it is feeling comfortable and relaxed. A brief recollection from earlier in the day, nothing of consequence.

Such a lovely June evening, almost sultry. The sliding glass doors of my houseboat were wide open onto the side facing the river. I had taken to sitting there after dinner to enjoy a leisurely cup of coffee while watching the implacable current of the River Thames; thoughts would eventually ebb and flow along with it. With my free hand I was absently stroking Gollum, my elderly black cat where he lay wrapped around himself and heavy in my lap. Obviously it was doing this that had reminded me.

Earlier that day a man had come round to cut two holes into the steel hull. I had decided to remove the full-sized bath tub and replace it with a shower stall. He had been recommended by a neighbour as someone who was happy to take on odd jobs for the sort of modest payment I could afford.

I heard him arrive in his pick-up truck, as did the rest of Wraysbury if the rattling noise of it was anything to go by. I watched through the window as he struggled down the slope of the garden with a cylinder each of acetylene and oxygen. They were strapped to a rusty sack barrow of the sort normally used to haul bags of cement and sand. Both he and the barrow trembled with the effort. The contraption was well past its serviceable life and moved like some supermarket trolleys do, preferring to wobble to left or right than forward. Fortunately, the man was tall and built large enough to insist. He came through the door breathless but grinning.

'Hello,' he said. 'I'm Ken.'

'Thank you for coming.' I replied politely. 'I didn't realise that you would need so much gear, would you like a cup of tea before you start?'

'Please,' he answered.

His voice was bass, the accent 'Bow Bells' cockney. He perched himself on one of the stools at the long strip of counter that separated the galley from the rest of the saloon. Not a shy person, I decided. He looked even bigger close up. His thick unruly hair met his beard in equal proportions so that without his bright eyes and ready smile he might have appeared a bit wild. I decided that a prim approach was the most prudent until I had the measure of him.

Gollum, disgruntled at having his evening routine disturbed, sniffed at the intruder's feet. Ken looked down then slowly extended his arm, half curling his fingers slowly so that Gollum could touch them with his nose – the only way to make polite acquaintance with a cat.

Before I could make a move to distract Gollum, knowing well that not everyone is enchanted by cats, Ken had joined him on the floor. Tickled his tummy, baby talked, smoothed and flattened his ears, rubbed that erogenous zone in felines which lies under the very tip end of their chins.

Several minutes passed. His tea was cold. I began to feel embarrassed about such mutual passion taking place on the floor of my galley. Huge hands, I noticed, calloused and dirt stained. There was nothing about it you could stab at with a pencil, but a tiny sadness surfaced, together with a small nudge of jealousy.

'Er ... shall I show you the bathroom?'

'Oh yes, better get on.' Giving Gollum a final head to tip of tail stroke, he rose to his feet.

'I like cats,' he said simply.

It didn't take long to cut the two holes and £5 was such a

reasonable price. I could do the rest myself. I didn't tell him that though. I'd once changed the fuse in an electric plug in front of a boyfriend.

'Why didn't you ask me to do that!' His voice had been aggrieved. Since then I had learned to be careful about such massive skills. He didn't last long: his chauvinism went way beyond plugs and fuses.

I made more tea, we chatted for a while as he set the cylinders back onto the trolley. I cannot remember a single word of that conversation but never forgot the way he was with Gollum.

It was the first note of the song of course, something coming, something good. Curious thing love, happening as it so often does as randomly as an egg is fertilised only to be viewed later, when the birth comes, as fatefully ordained.

Ken was a well-known character in the area, 'character' as in village vernacular. His name featured often in the meaningful gossip, the daily bulletins that so enliven a small neighbourhood. Nothing malicious. Everyone knew his vehicle; even if they could not read a number-plate from the prescribed distance they would recognise his fly-away hair from afar. All agreed that he had never been seen in a suit. Clever with his hands, they reckoned: the sort of handyman everyone likes to 'know' of; a man who will repair the clutch, get that 40-year-old tractor going again, build a house, plumb in the new sink or the central heating. The type that will do it for very little. If he felt like it he sometimes wouldn't charge a penny, you never knew.

I didn't know that the first note had sounded. Just as well, too – it would have been disappointing, perhaps even spoiled it. The best part of a concert is the tingling anticipation that builds as the orchestra is warming up, drowning out the last coughs and shuffles in the audience, the baton rising, the nod of the conductor, silence, and now ... begin!

Anyway, it was through gossip and storytelling that I first felt a connection with him. The best of these concerned his job as the security officer and part-time groundsman at the local cricket club…

The small group of seven- to nine-year-olds had baited and teased the cricket club members for more than a year and the problem was a regular item on the agenda of the committee meetings. During this time the subject had nevertheless served some pretty useful, if disguised, purposes. Those most vehement in denouncing the committee for their apparent powerlessness in dealing with the problem felt better afterwards about their exclusion from the playing team or their position in the batting order. It was always a more eloquent debate than that which concerned the leak in the changing rooms. There were splendid opportunities for pronouncements about the state of the country and for personal recollections of an impeccable youth.

The 'gang' had established its notoriety through deliberate acts of petty vandalism: breaking windows in the club house, using the cricket creases as goal lines in their games of football. The very first attempt at deterrence, that of waving bats and fists in the air, had set the rules of the war game, which resulted in a disadvantage from which the cricketers never recovered. First of all, it looked ridiculous and, secondly, it advertised to both sides the superior weaponry of the lads who could outrun and outcurse even the number one bat who had a reputation for both these accomplishments.

All in all, however, the irritation caused by the activities of the boys was not intolerable and in time was even absorbed into the ethos of the club. Most members felt that the lads would grow out of it over time. Indeed many of the oaths exchanged had a strong element of banter to them. Outstanding examples of such wit were applauded on both sides. There were even rare moments of alliance such as occurred one well-remembered Saturday. The visiting team's fast bowler had an awesome reputation. At the moment of his first delivery the lads had thrown themselves to the ground in mock fear. The visiting captain complained and duly received a very adequate, totally insincere apology. As a result the home team suffered only a resounding defeat, which compared favourably with pre-match predictions about an embarrassing annihilation.

The local Bobby attended the next match and was seen to approach the boys at the edge of the field. Nothing could be heard of the lecture he delivered but the gestures were appropriate. He stood before the lads, helmet very straight, poked his index finger at each of them in turn. He left immediately afterwards with a wave of completion towards the pavilion.

The following day the creases were found to be saturated with engine oil and at the next committee meeting the subject of the gang headed the agenda. The outcome was a vote for a practical course of action. Other solutions were offered at the same meeting but were dismissed in turn as being either final, sadistic or illegal! One young player suggested that the boys be given the opportunity to practise with the players at the nets but although the idea earned a debate it was eventually turned down because the net facilities were already at a premium, even the cause of some unsightly quarrels between members. Finally, it was decided that a caravan be sited in a corner of the field to accommodate a groundsman and caretaker.

The applicants were interviewed carefully. The final choice fell on a man with a full dark beard who stood well over six feet tall. He was not asked his age but was obviously in the prime of his life. He had a distinctive way of walking, a measured rhythmic style, suggesting that hesitation of either step or mind was unusual in him. He was told there might be a problem with a few of the local lads.

That spring the boys had discovered a new pastime. They were roving the perimeter of the pitch collecting birds eggs. The caretaker came upon them suddenly as the five huddled round their diminutive leader comparing their finds. A blackbird was loud and close by uttering confused quavers of alarm call. The boys stared at the man cautiously. He continued his step without pausing and joined them on his haunches. Looking at the eggs they had collected, he remarked that the larger ones were blackbirds' eggs. Four heads turned towards the leader and waited urgently.

Holding the stranger's gaze, the leader carefully put his hand into the right pocket of his jeans with a slight swagger.

'I found those,' he said deliberately. Accepting the words at face value, the man nodded then asked him what he was going to do with them.

'Keep them,' the young man shrugged.

'You'll have to blow them first,' his lieutenant dared.

The leader rounded on him, 'I know that, stupid!'

A device for picking stones out from horses' hooves was produced from a pocket. The tall stranger stayed with them while the holes were made at each end of the egg. It was then passed to the leader who began to blow. A bloody droplet of mucus appeared and began to stretch towards the ground. The lad strained, red in the face, but brushed hands off that wanted to help. The man murmured that it might be a bit late in the season.

'What do you mean?' asked the lad, pausing to summon more breath.

The tall, bearded caretaker answered them. 'Well, let's see how it goes.'

The egg suddenly split open. A roar of disappointment went up, drowning for a brief moment the unrelenting protests of the female blackbird. The cause of the failure plopped onto the grass in a mire of bloody strands and yolk. The foetus was well developed with a shading of feathers down its back, the beak bright and fleshy but closed. The boys didn't like it and didn't know what to say. They looked to the man.

'That's a shame,' he said before covering the lumpy wetness with grass and twigs.

He then told them that he had found a thrush's nest nearby and planned to take some photographs in the hope of catching the eggs as they hatched and then recording the development of the fledglings, though he wasn't too hopeful of being around at the right time.

The tallest lad with the punk hairstyle spoke up this time. The leader tolerated his impudence and remained silent.

'Where is this thrush's nest then?' The man they would come to know as Ken smiled at them all. Before he spoke again he absentmindedly put some more twigs on the grave.

'If I show you where it is and you take the eggs, I won't be able to photograph them, and besides, I like birds.'

He got up as if to go then but he had impressed them somehow. They didn't want him to leave.

'We can find the nests and then tell you where they are if you like.'

The volunteer was the fat boy who only maintained his gang membership in exchange for constant taunts about his size and cowardice. Realising that his suggestion had earned general approval, his excitement was a sad thing to observe. He squirmed, clenching his fists tightly to his sides. He badly wanted to feel again the warming surge it gave to his body but his further comments threatened the dignity of the gang and he was told firmly to shut up.' He did so, but from now on he would risk himself again.

Ken then said, 'We will have to take care that the birds are not disturbed. Because I'm big I tend to make too much noise, which could discourage the birds from completing their nests or, worse, cause the females to desert the nest.' He then left them while he fetched his camera, promising to return shortly. When he got back to the place he could see no sign of the boys until the leader popped his head up in triumph followed by the four others.

Ken called out to them, 'That's it, that's the way!'

The leader made this first project his personal responsibility, explaining through his own plans the standard he required from the rest of them.

'I'm going to come here three times a day and let him know when the first eggs are laid. If I see anyone else come near this nest, you'll get it!' He added a full stop with his clenched fist. The other four set off to find their own nests and territory to guard.

During the following days and weeks, five nests were carefully and conscientiously monitored. The caravan became a tea station. A notebook was used to record species, number of eggs, sequence of laying. The fat boy excelled: he even managed to record how many times the starlings were fed in one day. He admitted that he had fallen asleep for an hour but asked the man whether an average was OK based on the previous hours. When he was told that it was the scientific way of doing things, the boy felt again that acute swell of pleasure. His mother worried about him getting up at five in the mornings.

The new groundsman and caretaker was called out as often as eight times a day to take photographs. He took to wearing his camera round his neck as he drove the tractor mower around the outfield. The club games were played thereafter without any interference from the lads. The fat boy won the hobbies prize at his school for an 'outstanding and meticulous study'. Mick was the smallest of the group. While the others eventually moved on to other interests, he became Ken's shadow. He had found his significant person in life and in time was all but his adopted son – mine too.

Other things were said about Ken. Divorced, two kids, had a 'cracking' girlfriend; not married, though, you know, such a scruffy bloke, nice enough though. They had no idea that they were paying him compliments when they talked like that. It all sounded like wholesome integrity to me. I, for one, wanted to know him.

They said, too, that he was building a boat. 'He'll never do it,' said the executives and accountants and the neighbours. 'He's the security man, lives in a caravan, bit of a gypsy if you ask us, middle aged, no money in the bank, build a sailing yacht? From scratch? Nonsense! What a dreamer!

Chapter 2

For eight years Ken had lived with Helen in the caravan at the cricket club. Younger than he by 15 years, she was attractive, ambitious, neat and tidy. Life with Ken was loving and caring but not always dynamic. It was still early spring in her life and like a catkin loaded with pollen she was ready for the right wind to blow. A talented young woman with fine secretarial skills, she was neither tested nor fulfilled in such a narrow environment. She bravely determined to go to America. There was talk of getting Ken a job there but for a man who had so far negotiated every aspect of life on his own terms the idea of being organised was not a comfortable one.

'I've always wanted to build a boat. I'll do it now. When it's finished I will come to America. I'll sail across.'

Despite many months working on the boat, both to prove his intent and to raise her opinion of him, there had been no change of heart. Helen was successful in America. As weeks passed, then seasons, it became clear that she would not resume her life with Ken. It was equally clear that however nice an apartment may be, a place without a tool shed was not the environment for him.

The caravan, which had for so long vibrated with comings and goings, was now a spent and empty place. It was particularly hard for a man who so enjoyed the company of women. He was not a social person. There was no solace for him in a pub, on a dinner date or at a party where he might have found comfort if not passion. Middle age is a difficult time for circumstances like that. Women found him attractive because he was so attentive, so ready to engage with them emotionally. Perhaps, too, because he was unconventional in other ways that were equally intriguing:

he made no pretence of the fact that he needed sexual solace, that it was oxygen to him, though he expressed this need in a way that was respectful and courteous. Boyish, a knight who could only afford wooden armour, a Just William, a handsome gypsy, a man for whom most women will make an exception! Ardent and enthusiastic as an adolescent, he was at the same time solicitous and kind. Yet he was also capable of selfishness, indifference and frequent terrible rages. It was a recipe that women were prepared to try out, perhaps because it never suggested anything more complicated than a respite from whatever dissatisfactions bothered them, carried no threat as far as children and husbands were concerned, or to comfortable lives fuelled by workaholic husbands. But it was lonely in the end.

And so it was, with wide open eyes and mutual caution, that we began our middle-aged love affair. There was very little lightning about it and hardly any blindness. Ken was still grieving for someone else. He was also the least romantic person I had ever met. I was not looking for anything more than I already had ... yet he was so easy to be with, so able to talk about anything and everything ... so glad of home-cooked meals.

It was 1979. We spent most of that summer together. By Christmas of 1980 I knew that I loved him though it was not a subject that either of us touched on. We just grew together like a couple of saplings planted at the same time, in the same place, in the same wood.

I knew he was building a boat. He mentioned it sometimes.

'Can't think of anything nicer than a cosy two-berth cabin cruiser, especially at twilight on the River Thames. I'm in a generous mood today so I am even prepared to lend you my junior hacksaw, set square and rubber-handled claw-hammer.' I said this while peeling potatoes, a task better suited to coy remarks than serious conversation. But it was not rivers or cabin cruisers that Ken was seeing in his mind. It was oceans.

'Actually it's a forty-foot, steel, sea-going yacht ... with sails!' said Ken.

I was astounded. 'How silly of me. You'll need at least three hacksaws for a job like that!'

I simply hadn't understood. As I got to know him better I came to realise the enormity of his undertaking. There was a good deal more to it all than the obvious physical demands or simply following technical data about welding, dimensions, or the best way to lay in ballast. It was to be a triumph of determination, a masterpiece of do-it-yourself that would embrace every conceivable practical skill.

Even to have constructed the bare skeleton of his boat was a Herculean achievement for a man on his own. It took weeks just to transfer each line drawing in the flimsy plans onto heavy duty wallpaper. There were three angles to calculate on each of 23 pairs of ribs, each measured with a protractor before being written up.

The winter of 1978/9 had been persistently cold. Every night of it had been spent in the unheated shed. Sometimes Mick would come and spend an evening. He was still in short trousers then – he would be a man by the time of the launch. Since the day he had met Ken at the boundary of the cricket club when they blew the bird's egg, their relationship had developed to become one that would be envied by every father, every son.

In one corner of the shed the large figure of Ken could be seen bending over the engineer's vice, in another, the diminutive figure of young Mick huddled next to the arm saw. They talked about the boat, Mick's troubles at home where he was pig-in-the-middle between an alcoholic father and a bullying older brother: the general complicated business of growing up.

The shed was barely two metres by three. By early January of 1979 it was packed to the roof with sufficient numbered pieces of steel to make up a 40-foot steel hull. The schedule Ken had imposed on himself was both punishing and unrelenting. The reality of it all had become a very solid object. Whatever part romantic illusion may have played in it all ended right then.

Locating the boat-yard site at Shepperton served to rekindle the enthusiasm somewhat. It was a small yard near the lock, less than a hundred metres from the River Thames. Within a day, Ken laid in his own 30 amp power supply and meter. Then, using a borrowed truck, he made several trips a day, loading and unloading. A week later the enormous proportions of a fat-bellied 40-foot skeleton made a strikingly resolute appearance in the yard.

She rose from the ground. As she did so the energy drained from Ken's hands.

The boat would languish in this state for nearly a year, looking ugly and at the same time strangely beautiful: a dormant grub waiting to begin its wriggling struggle against overwhelming odds, and live. Yet it was not the burden of work that had drained Ken's energy. It was the motivation that was all wrong. He was himself a stricken vessel lying broadside and rudderless in big seas – an emotional storm raged inside him.

I didn't understand that Ken's turmoil was as much to do with his boat as with the ending of his relationship. It was haunting him.

He was 44 years old. When he counted up all the money he possessed it came to £300, just enough to buy a set of plans, the first few tons of steel. With no further capital, nor promise of any, everything would be 'build as you earn', make what you cannot afford to buy. He had never sailed a boat in his life – not even a dinghy.

Yet his dream was still to build an ocean going yacht, then sail it across the Atlantic. It was an absurd position to start from. There was nothing at all on which to base a belief that he could succeed. Surely not even will power and optimism could overcome such obstacles.

* * *

Having no special significance in Ken's life at that particular time, other than as part-time companion and provider of a roast dinner on Sundays, I was not the person he went to for solace. Besides which, matters of pride or self-doubt are sometimes better shared man to man or woman to woman as they generally are.

Ken's best mate was Richard. They had met as fellow patients in hospital. Both engineering types, they were having traction treatment for slipped discs caused by lugging heavy weights around – carelessly, they both admitted ruefully. Instant friendship. The sort you know will last. Bane of nurses though, both of them: too familiar by far, frustrated by the inactivity, impatient, fretful, cheeky, talked incessantly about engines when they had been told over and over not to move even an eyebrow.

Richard had built up his own small but specialised engineering business maintaining and installing industrial valves. He was dry, dour and cynical. A professional devil's advocate who was all heart and soul though he would pretend to hate you if you dared suggest so. He never said the things you would expect from a friend; anyone who didn't know him would have cringed.

There was Ken, putting himself out there, talking of sadness and failure, and Richard would shrug, or roll his eyes or smirk. Then he would say, 'Never mind ... water under the bridge ... what are you worried about? Nothing.' Outrageous counsellor! But it worked. Like confrontational therapy, it worked. You and your boat are small potatoes in the bigger scheme of things, just decide what you want to do about it and get on with it, the universe won't change one little bit whether you do or you don't! No place for woolly thinking with Richard. He was a great fan of the reality curve.

But Richard knew Ken, understood the problem he was facing, and he did care. Which was why he was there on the day that really mattered. A day when an intimate friend aims to get the timing just right.

Ken had spent the whole day at the boat-yard. He'd been there from early morning, not doing much, just thinking. Against the backdrop of a now darkening sky, the skeleton of the boat looked just like a wreck stranded on a reef, decks and superstructure already corroded away, only the sad bones of the ship left over now to be gnawed at by the surf. The metaphor for disaster was not lost on Ken.

A van swerved into the yard and scrunched to a halt on the gravel... Ken had already adjusted the ratio of oxygen to acetylene. As the headlights of the van illuminated his figure he lit the flame. He turned to see Richard approaching. When Ken spoke there was neither determination nor relief in his voice. It was worse than that – something much closer to despair.

'I'm going to cut it up, Richard, my heart's not in it any more.'

Richard ignored the words. He moved in gently to take the gas cutter from his friend's hands.

'You'll only regret it, mate. Come on, we'll go and have a cuppa.'

Both grips increased slightly. Their eyes met in feigned challenge. A frozen moment passed between them before Ken's hand relaxed and he allowed himself to be led away.

'What brought you round, Richard?'

'Just passing, mate ... just passing.'

From Ken: 'There will always be a berth for you, Richard ... there ... whenever you have need of it.' A man's way of saying thank you.

'Not much chance of that if you cut the bloody thing up!' smirked Richard.

It seems so strange now that 20 years have passed that it did not occur to either of us that we might tackle the project together; yet it was about that time, for reasons I shall never be sure of, that I resigned from the Probation Service. After 19 years of uninterrupted work at various jobs it was easy to rationalise that a six month 'sabbatical' would prepare me for what to do next. I was disappointed by the justice system and with the unrealistic expectations of society. Social workers pick up the pieces of blighted lives long after the damage has been done. The pain in people's lives is sometimes unbearable. Blame is then easily directed at social services instead of at the real perpetrators.

Giving up a well paid profession felt terribly risky. I was plagued by guilt for many months especially over the question of cowardice. If I didn't like what I saw, shouldn't I stay, try to change things? But I knew I did not have the personality for conflict or for activism so I withdrew. Would I become more delinquent still?

For the next three months I spent a lot of time wondering what on earth had possessed me. If someone had suggested then that I was about to exchange my court suit for a boiler suit or one day pose naked across the cab of a fork-lift truck I would, as they say, have laughed them out of court.

Work on the boat continued at an even, if reluctant, pace. Ken was now a very frequent visitor and the atmosphere was easy between us, but I also knew that the building of his boat was still in serious jeopardy. Unless I could find a way to encourage him, there could be no future for us together. Caring for a man who feels he has failed is very hard work. I did not feel that strong.

And then one night Ken told me of an event that captured my imagination in a way that nothing else ever had. It was only then that I fully understood what he was about and why it mattered so. By the time he had finished telling me the story both our lives had changed.

Chapter 3

The large field that was leased to the cricket club was once part of a sizeable country estate situated on the outskirts of Egham, in Berkshire. It was an ancient fiefdom, existing even before the time when cattle were herded along the rutted High Street in Staines.

Some time before the two wars, when the future looked as predictable as the past had always been, one of the gardeners planted a row of trees, impeccably spaced, along each of the boundaries. Less than 80 years later, all that remained of the estate were two small patches of green now used as playing fields. Of the hundreds of trees, the only remnant was a short line of oaks that skirted the pavilion boundary.

Berkshire is an oak tree county. At 80 years old these trees were mere saplings compared to their cousins in Windsor Great Park. Some of those gnarled giants are reputed to be 800 years old.

It happened during an ordinary summer squall. One of the young oak trees suddenly fell out of line like a fainting guardsman. Ken surveyed the scene next morning. There was a crater where it had been wrenched from the ground. The roots were still flailing in the subsiding wind. It was a stirring image of the sad kind.

An elderly man walked slowly across the field to join Ken at the scene. He was an ex-forester and had the laconic style of many outdoors people. He had a two-handed axe tucked under his arm, light as a baton, cosy as a hen resting a leg under its wing. He considered for a moment the fallen giant.

'Strange,' he said, scratching his neck with the peak of his cap. 'You want the trunk, lad?'

Ken nodded.

'Mind if I take the branches?'

'Help yourself,' smiled Ken.

The old man wielded his axe with a well practised efficiency. Within an hour he had cut and trimmed all the branches. Now he laid them neatly to one side. He would bring his hand cart round later.

Meanwhile, Ken was measuring the length and girth of the trunk and converting it to cubic feet. Here were the beams and furniture for the inside of his boat. To him it was a happy coincidence. To my ears it sounded more like an omen – trees don't normally fell themselves so conveniently.

Ken would remember the parting words from the old man. As he shouldered his axe to leave he remarked, 'She'll bleed.'

For six months the tree lay where it had fallen while Ken tried to figure out how he might get it to a sawmill. Now he was telling me about it. He'd come round two nights before looking desperately tired. There was sawdust in his hair. His hands looked raw and swollen. He had cut through the trunk once – ten solid hours – with a double-handed saw. Tomorrow he would do the same. And ten hours the day after that ... and the next.

When it fell, the top of the trunk touched higher ground so that it was lying at a slight angle. When the saw was about a third of the way through, a purple ink-like liquid began to bubble up between the teeth. It disturbed Ken. It was like cutting through living flesh. By the time he was finished some three gallons of 'blood' had spilled from the cut.

'He said it would bleed.'

We both felt that if the tree were given another 80 years of life by gracing the interior of a boat it might somehow expiate the uncomfortable feeling that a grave sin had been committed.

And there it was: contained within one tiny phase of the project, the meaning of the whole enterprise. It was not only about maximum effort, minimal cost, but also about a relationship between the builder and his materials. The boat took on a meaning for me then. Something too subtle to articulate, an echo perhaps, a resonance with my own past in the chrysalis years when I roamed and explored, when everything was made possible just by willing it so.

Each evening I listened with fascination to what was happening with the tree. After the fourth cut Ken used chains, the club tractor, and brute force to drag the timber to a lorry, then he drove off with it to the sawmill. By repairing the firm's belt saw over a few days he earned for his labour full preparation of the oak tree into 50 quarter-sawn planks. Arrangements like that still flourish. They rank amongst the most scrupulous and honourable of dealings between men. If there was a matter of surplus or deficit either way no one seemed to mind. The planks were laid up with meticulous care. Separating fillets of wood allowed the air to circulate. With the help of a few turns it seasoned away for four years.

By early spring of 1981 most of the hull plating had been tacked into position. The boat had now 'taken shape' as they say. A very dangerous time for such ventures. Now came the second and last crisis about her survival, this time the very knife edge, the do or die.

Over the following few weeks Ken and Richard probably drank enough tea to fill the hull. Those who knew Ken waited. Those who didn't nodded kindly and remembered similar ventures that had achieved the rank of 'good tries'.

Finally he came to me.

'I'm going to cut it up.'

A deep ache started up inside me. I felt utterly confused. It wasn't as if he had said, 'I'm going to cut it up because...' What was I to do with such a blank statement?

Did he want me to console him, tell him that never mind, it was the right decision, or should I be urging him to keep going? Why was he telling me this? More than that, why was it hurting so much?

I knew it wasn't just the prospect of three quarters of a mile of up-hand, down-hand, horizontal, vertical, lie on your side and feel your way welding; though that in itself is a fair test of anyone's grit and temperament. He was well enough into the project by now to realise what the demands on him would be.

We stared at each other. Whoever spoke next would be saying something very important between us. Words now waiting to be said could never be taken back, never put right if they were wrong.

We backed off for a moment.

'How do you see things, Pat, how do you see the world?' asked Ken.

It seemed an odd question but I answered with an enthusiasm that surprised me. I leaned forward and touched his face.

'Me? I'll tell you. I own the world. I was born on this spiral galaxy quite randomly, just another good egg, yards from where we are sitting give or take a few hundred miles, which is nothing really. Then I became a caterpillar and played the odds, learned things.'

I was speaking in a rush now because I now knew what I was going to say and was not afraid of any consequences.

'I'm going to prove that the same thing can happen all over again.'

'What?!' said Ken.

'You'll do it. You'll build your boat and then you will sail it to wherever you want to go.'

It was while I was speaking my own riddle to him that I realised that the man I had come to love was asking me to give him a reason for going on. It was the most charming piece of emotional blackmail I had ever encountered – if the boat foundered then so would we.

That, then, was how I made the best and most extraordinary decision of my life. How I might help wasn't at all clear, but whatever else, I resolved to go with him to the boat-yard the very next day. Not just to visit but to do.

We would work together and live together 24 hours a day from that moment on. The boat had two beginnings so perhaps it was appropriate that she would have two endings: the journey to America to fulfil the promise; and our own destination after that.

The boat was bigger than both of us then. By the end we would be bigger than the boat – the right way round.

Chapter 4

'Take this, love. Grind off the excess steel where it comes through from the side decks.'

'Right, Ken.'

I put out both arms to cradle the monstrous gadget that was being handed to me so casually. It was about 900 times heavier than it looked. My height is 'national average' according to the statistics: 1.69 metres. I wear size four shoes and weigh in at 120 pounds on an average dry day, give or take an ounce.

The added weight instantly descended to my hips. Failing to dislocate them, it transferred to those more vulnerable joints in my knees. These buckled together quickly enough and noisily enough to satisfy most forms of belligerent intent.

Having a streak of British in me, I did manage to stagger about and maintain balance rather than kneel before some pushy angle grinder. I gazed hard at Ken's receding back. He would turn around, admit he was kidding. He didn't ... he wasn't!

Right then! Using up the first flush of calories from my breakfast cereal, I managed, through means that now elude me, to climb the ladder into the boat where I plugged the thing into the extension lead. The jagged edges of the steel plate were well above my head so I employed some of the initiative that arrives with middle age and found a bucket to stand on – so far so good, girl! I then discovered that the wretched goggles that Ken had draped around my neck were too loose. After I had tied a knot in them they were too tight!

Having at last managed all these preliminary procedures I was finally ready to start work. Clutching the beast to my chest, I pressed the starter button. The equivalent of eight bags of sugar vibrated into action with a stupefying noise. It then proceeded to arm wrestle at 6,000 revolutions a minute.

Any notion of grinding off surplus metal was a hopelessly forlorn objective. The best I could achieve was a muscle-binding stalemate, a sort of basic control over the monster until my knuckles became white unto gangrene.

Too weak by now to carry the angle grinder back down the ladder, I left it next to the puddle of sweat and made a slow and wobbly descent to ground level. I felt foolish and embarrassed. The very first task on the very first day; if this was my best effort at so-called help and encouragement, it was pathetic. At least it presented the opportunity for splendid understatement. Rather ruefully, I said, 'I don't think I can manage that!'

I suppose I expected lots of tuts, deep sighs, imploring looks to heaven, but Ken simply suggested that I might like to tidy up a bit and what about a cup of tea? Here we go, I thought, this is how it will be: sweeping up, making tea and sandwiches. Then again, perhaps he had noticed that I had been missing for an hour, that beads of sweat were still breaking out like a rash of pimples on my face.

It would be a recurring problem. Ken has a frame that would match seven feet as well as it does his six feet two. Men who are built like dredgers never adjust to the fact that female orang-utans have a slighter form.

It would have been a very disappointing end to our first working day together if Ken hadn't bothered to take time out in setting up the equipment so that I could try my hand at welding. He showed me how to lodge the rod in the holder then strike the arc. After providing me with various bits of scrap metal to join together, he left me to it. After a couple of hours I had managed several flat welds and one passable gusset weld. That modest success cheered me up considerably. We shared our first end of the day smiles together.

As we packed up to leave, several wedges of Canada geese flew low over the boat-yard. Every spring and autumn evening they timed their departure with ours. Noisy, gossiping, quarrelling birds. They were headed towards their dormitories at the gravel pits while we headed towards a hot meal and to rest whichever part of us ached the most. We knew that they mated for life and somehow their regular appearance came to symbolise our commitment to each other and the project. It was as if they were checking in on us.

For the rest of that first week I helped where I could and made frequent mugs of tea and hod-loads of sandwiches. At all other times I was busy in the apprentice's corner welding bits of metal – Tate Gallery quality some of it – then a good bash and bong with the club hammer to check that they were sound.

By the second week I was welding on the boat, joining the decking to the hull. All straightforward down-hand work where any mistakes are easily ground out. In some places there were quite large gaps. The technique here was to fill them with several short rows of weld. I needed approval.

'This is a bit more than you would normally expect from a first-year apprentice you know.'

'By the time you can fill a hole the size of a two pence piece you will be halfway to calling yourself a welder,' said Ken, raising his eyebrows in case I thought of contradicting what he was saying.

'Not bad, though?'

'Not bad.' And I knew he meant it.

I was so keen to earn the accolade of 'halfway a welder' that by the second week I was filling holes with even a hint of a flourish. Every one a challenge. I pounced on them like a hungry cat.

It highlighted a difference in our temperaments that we would only later learn to use constructively. When something went wrong for Ken he would bellow and curse like a madman, throw things, generally behave as though this current frustration was the last he would ever tolerate. While all that was going on, and in those days it happened several times a day, I would be kneeling in a concentrated hunch over the same wretched hole until I felt totally sure that it was filled to its proper depth of metal. I put a lot of that patience down to the beastly angle grinder – fewer errors, less grinding out to do. Although it was marginally easier to use in the down-hand mode, it still hated me as much as I detested it.

The nostalgia we feel now about those bright uneven days has a special flavour. My own optimism about the success of the venture was born of ignorance, but when the enormity of the task became clearer it was those early months of learning to trust and understand each other that would sustain us for the next seven years.

On days when the thought of welding for yet another ten hours was too daunting to face, Ken made one-off items like the chain plates. He upgraded most of the specifications recommended in the plans. Strength was an obsession with him. Where boats are concerned it was the right attitude. Every deck fitting was backed up by a larger plate of steel fully welded to the deck head to spread the load between the frames. The chain plates would carry the standing rigging. If they ever failed, it could only be the result of an unimaginable catastrophe that would first have ripped off the deck!

Jobs like that made a welcome change from some of the more tedious work. Consolidating the ribs was a colossal bore. Small triangles of metal to reinforce each of the angles. Twenty-three on the starboard side, another twenty-three on the port side. A person on their own might easily give up in disgust.

Just in time to boost our spirits, Richard offered the unconditional loan of a second welder. He did so in his inimitable way.

'What, you here again?' To me. 'Following him around like a shadow, seems to me. I'm not using this at the moment. Don't you go using it, you'll break it.' Then he chucked his chin in the air, stayed for a mug of tea, and set the welder up for me to use.

It was a fine gesture and a great help. I became totally possessive about that welder. Well, it was Richard and I loved him dearly, besides it's impossible to 'break' a welder without the use of a missile. I regarded it as entirely 'mine for the use of' as they say in military circles. It made me feel that I belonged to the project despite all the early misgivings.

We were meticulous about the welding. Whenever we felt the slightest doubt we ground it out to have a look. Even a tiny pinhole could lead to a reservoir of slag. No wonder slag is such a rude word. Had I known its origins before, I would have thought it ruder still. A horrible lava of residue from the flux of the arc rod that must be painstakingly chipped out.

Summer arrived. Now the welding was a foretaste of Satan's domain. We were obliged to wear sweaters and boiler suits to protect against the ultraviolet light. It can cause severe burns. I was horrified to learn that it can also make you hairy! The hot slag posed a constant danger. Several times a day a lump of it would jump into a pocket, or much worse, a wellington boot. It would then smoulder away maliciously. Quite soon after that one of us would 'do the dance'. At the flapping arm stage it looks like skydiving with flares at ground level. It was also truly amazing how often we forgot that recently welded areas stay scalding hot for a long time. The pain doesn't seem to reach the brain until the burn is second degree!

To relieve the monotony of so much welding and to give our lungs a break, we would spend a few days at a time making the mast and bowsprit fittings, the bollards, the Samson post. Buying those items, or paying to have them made, can cost several hundred pounds. Fortunately, even the best engineers make cock-ups, enabling the likes of us to collect largish quantities of mild steel plate and tubing that had been scrapped just because a hole was drilled in the wrong spot.

All these finished pieces were sent away for hot-dipped galvanising. Some would not be handled again for more than five years, but they were there when we needed them at a time in the future when our physical resources were nearly exhausted.

The next skill for me to master was gas cutting. We could then work independently and make much better progress. By late summer we were up to the bulwarks.

The main attraction for me at the end of that first six months was in seeing Ken so alive and energetic again. We were completely comfortable with each other by then; the atmosphere between us was warm and stimulating. Yet he could be aggravatingly intolerant too. The maxim 'once shown never forgotten' may have come easily to him but my progress was more in the order of 'once shown I may have to be reminded a few times.'

But wasn't I supposed to be helping for a bit and then deciding what direction to take with my career? Just a bit longer, I thought, just until I can decide.

Together we cut the cardboard templates for the bulwarks to follow the curve of the deck. Each time we tacked a new bit onto the boat the effect was dramatic. Then followed the interminable welding ... this was all going to be a very long haul indeed.

The plans suggested that the bulwarks be capped out with flat steel bar then covered by a wooden rail, but Ken decided it was not the character he was after. He would never be casual about essential maintenance to do with mechanics and rigging but he was not comfortable with the idea of annual varnishing or pre-season prettying. He rarely looked at the plans from then on.

He decided on good old gas barrel steel and bought it in 20-foot lengths. The problem then confronting us was how to follow the curves that are so much a part of the boat's traditional lines. A huge frame of scaffolding we found lying in the yard solved the problem. Leverage was the answer. Ken fed the tube across the frame, a few inches at a time while I did a prehensile bit on the other end. By exaggerating the bend, it allowed for the amount of distortion caused by heat when we cut the incision that would feed it onto the plate. Tacked into position, it added a nice finished appearance to the bulwarks as well as giving them immense strength. Ken always took pains to describe engineering theory and practice and would often ask for my opinion. At first I thought he was doing it just to jolly me along, some psychological device to make me feel like an equal contributor. Not so. He genuinely assumed I would be interested. I was. Sometimes I had to stop him going into too much detail but I was surprised at how much would stick and become useful years later when we could ponder such questions together on more equal terms. The end of each small phase of the project was a matter for celebration. A time to stand back, even briefly, and relish a feeling of genuine progress.

Perhaps it was those smooth rails highlighting the symmetrical sweep of her length and beam? Or perhaps it was when any lingering doubts about the boat's destiny for the sea were finally dispelled? Whatever it was, on a memorable day towards the end of that autumn the boat became a living thing – a distinct personality.

That may sound a little anthropomorphic, but most of the folk we met who regularly went to sea, and even those who didn't, were not particularly shy in admitting that it was their craft that seduced *them*, rather than the other way round.

I was washing my hands in a corner of the boat-yard. I happened to look back at the boat. Ken was leaning his head against the cold steel, both arms outstretched in an attitude of embrace. I looked away quickly, not from embarrassment, but from feeling like the third party. My hands proved to be dirtier than I thought: they needed washing a second time, a third time.

He was talking quietly. And I knew he was already sailing her, trusting her in a force nine gale, sharing the desperate moments of anxiety about what in essence had become a mutual obligation – he and his craft promising to try.

If it is quite all right for an artist to weep over his or her canvas, for the sculptor to embrace the granite, then it is quite OK for a boiler-suited boat-builder, too.

If the boat had at last become 'she', then she was a big woman, broad in the beam. Even the contrasting sleekness in the lines of her prow could never make her the capricious aristocrat, more the earth-wise Demeter figure. Ken had chosen to model her on a Bruce Roberts 'Spray', a larger replica of the vessel in which Joshua Slocum made the first solo circumnavigation of the globe. The boat they had all said was too heavy and broad to succeed in such an endeavour.

Whatever it was that happened that day between Ken and his creation, it needed to happen. Only a total commitment would see them through the tough times that lay ahead.

Chapter 5

Mother was now in her late eighties. I took time out for my autumn visit with her.

Over the last couple of years I'd noticed that she had shrunk a little more each time I saw her. Her day dresses hung loosely from her shoulders, flattened breasts hardly giving any contour to the fabric. She looked brittle and frail. When I hugged her it was slowly and carefully as if she might crumble away in my arms. I wanted to tell her what was happening, needed to put it in a way that would make her happy for me.

'I've met a nice man, mum, he's building a boat.'

'I hope he's kind to you, Pat … has he got a good job?'

'He works very hard, mum.'

'Oh good … that's always good … your dad was a hard worker.' And that seemed enough for her.

I knew that part of her was gone from me. She had 'packed her bags', even said so once. 'I want to go you know, Pat … I'm ready to go.' She honoured me by saying that, knowing that she would not have to defend herself against platitudes. I had heard people sound angry when their parents spoke the truth: 'Don't talk like that! Take your pills! You must eat more!' How harsh it must sound to be chastened like that when you are old and know the score and should be free to say any damn thing you please! Children becoming tyrants – too sad by far and far.

It was as if she stood ready in the hall of her mind, gazing down the corridor at a door, a nicely painted, well kept door, that would soon open, let her pass, then close for ever behind her. She sat ready, unafraid, hands calmly folded in her lap. She joked about her 'busy leg' as she called it, which had scuffed a bald patch in the carpet at the foot of her chair, her balding head, the way her plate flopped about in her shrunken mouth. She looked at me with great tenderness as she said these things. I loved her enough to let her be.

Anyway the truth would only worry her. It had begun to worry me. I was working in a boat-yard every day, rarely combed my hair, no money, no career, no recreation, going in no particular direction that I could call my own.

We had a ritual at parting, in case it was goodbye.

'Do you still love me, mum?'

Her whole face smiled. 'Oh yes,' she would say, 'oh yes.' Never a need for me to reply.

'Crikey!' I thought as I drove back to Windsor. I'd chucked the boulder way down into the valley, was scampering after it but somehow never catching up with it. I would have to turn back. I'd run too far already and had entered an unfamiliar world only to find it recognisable, as if I had been born there. But that is no excuse, is it? There I was talking to myself in the car. Soon I must tell Ken that it was time for me to move on and, however reluctantly, find my way back.

But thank you. Thank you! I wish for you all that is good.

I must fend for myself in this life, can't go waltzing off like this, however much I might enjoy both the music and the dance. I must tell Ken that now he is back in the swing of things it is time for me to go.

But love, girl! Love. Wasn't that the ultimate goal of any life? Stupid, stupid! Grief, the number of women who follow a guy, and stumble, and he never looks back, and she calls it love. Battered and disregarded, worn out, dried up, and she calls it love. Unrequited love – what a bore – what a waste.

Getting scared now. But it is wintertime, not a good season for changing things. Spring is better. I will find my way back in the spring.

Chapter 6

The closing weeks of autumn 1981. The boat-yard was a different place, a quiet environment for a dedicated few. Gradually the busy clattering sounds of work, the high-pitched weekend voices, faded away. Men with paint brushes and beer cans, bikini-clad wives lying around the feet of ladders – all were gone. The long-neglected boats, abandoned boats, looked even more forlorn and friendless; some had waited more than 20 years for a summer visitor.

The few huddled together. Ken constructed a tent at the bow end of the boat to house the tools and to provide some respite from what turned out to be one of the harshest winters for many years. By mid-November nature herself had battened down the hatches. Even the bare trees seemed to hunch slightly, bracing themselves. Wild duck grouped together early to survive the ordeal in convoy.

We moved in the massive work bench made up from wooden pallets earlier in the year. One of the corners was a galley for the tea things and the sandwich toaster. With a circle of tea chests and the hedgerow for a curtain the tent became a cosy wigwam, providing shelter not only for ourselves but also for anyone else in the yard brave enough to confront that bitter winter.

Our journey to the boat-yard each day took us through the wandering approach roads into Chertsey village, with its dated shop-fronts, its far from London look. As we rounded one of the bends, we noticed some old and shabby furniture being thrown carelessly into a van.

'Chairs for the wigwam,' we shouted in unison. We sped along the pavement as fast as any two can in steel toe-capped boots.

Dressed as usual in miscellaneous layers of sweaters and balaclava scarves, we asked, in a polite and friendly way, could we have two of the armchairs please? The three lads stared at us without saying a word but they pointed at two that were a hideous orange.

'Ghastly colour,' I said.

'Character,' observed Ken.

'Very dirty.'

'You could make covers for them.' Withering look from me. One of my finest.

Triumphantly, we moved them into the shelter and ushered each other into the 'lounge'. Almost homely. I could barely resist the temptation to hang a picture on the privet hedge. It was agreed that might be a little over the top. Still, the chairs were enough to give that incongruous touch: one of the many bits of nonsense that rewarded us with precious moments of childlike delight. A couple of middle-aged adults learning how to frolic again.

Winter lunchtimes. On with the kettle and the toasted sandwiches. No one was asked to bring slices of cheese, eggs, corned beef, pilchards, but a fair rotation evolved in true democratic style.

There was something of a bygone age about those gatherings. If the talk was no longer about adzes and pin mauls it was still as ancient as the history of boats: pedestals and winches, sail configuration and rigs, mitres and scarf joints. In our motley assortment of winter garb, we stepped back in time. We might just as well have been a crew of Victorian workers. Here was crafts-manship, attention to detail, perseverance and the old-fashioned virtue of self-discipline. Without exception, we all preferred to have a boat as our taskmaster than some fretful executive. Only occasionally did the subjects of politics or beliefs crop up, usually because some fool had brought in a newspaper. Then the talk became louder and faster. But soon enough we would all revert once more to the rambling safety of non-committal boat talk.

We probably condensed 20 years of friendship into those couple of years before Chris left the yard and so changed the make-up of the group. He was a slim, engaging Irishman. Before volunteering for redundancy he had worked as an electronics wizard in the aircraft industry. He used the money to buy and fit out a 40-foot hull. He laboured away for nearly four years without once losing his dedication and was the first of the group to launch and sail his boat. His rhythm of working fitted the man; it was part of his shy stroll through life. A modest, charming man.

Early one morning we all hove to at the yard gates to watch him go. As the low loader manoeuvred through the gap, we knew we would miss him: our lunchtimes would never again be quite the same.

Mike was different. A dynamic purposeful young man with wide-ranging abilities. Building his boat was in his scheme of things. He challenged life. He approached his project with a tactician's mind suited to his army upbringing, and his efforts were quite simply heroic. His was also a 40-foot hull and he completed it at weekends and almost every evening, often until past midnight. It was impossible to tell with Mike whether he felt any affection towards his boat but his enthusiasm never flagged and no one ever doubted that he would succeed.

Mike was kind and thoughtful towards us, a good friend, but despite his warm soul he would not get close. In the emotional stakes, he wore a veneer of indifference, while everything he did gave lie to it.

Uncharacteristically, he was the least methodical and by far the most untidy worker of us all. Most of his tools lay buried under mounds of sawdust, chippings and offcuts. It was like a bran tub: to find a chisel try the lucky dip! His girlfriend would come down occasionally and insist on tidying up, couldn't help herself I suppose: we women always think it's the right thing to do then kid ourselves that we were only trying to help. You couldn't run a kitchen in that state, could you? We cringed when we saw her arrive. We would have to put up with Mike's grumbling about not being able to find a thing. Two whole days of it sometimes.

To cap these contradictions in his nature he would constantly chide us for our grubby ways. Before each break he scoured his mug and teaspoon with scrupulous care. Ken, whose own tea mug tended to last a week at a time, found this behaviour irresistible. He would wait for Mike to comment on the mixture of noxious substances adhering to the butter knife. Exactly on cue, he would proceed to wipe it carefully on a vaguely clean patch of his boiler suit before looking at Mike with a cherubic look on his face and a wicked twinkle in his eye. Dear Mike, he was terribly stern.

Des, like us, was in for the long haul. Maybe a decade of effort and financial hardship. Sometimes he'd become despondent or just plain weary about it all, but his boat kept calling – and he kept coming back. He had a pessimistic inclination, which he relieved with a witty, often self-deprecating humour. A small, robustly built man, yet with no trace of the self-conscious swagger that is sometimes to be found in men of small stature.

His wife Jan was even shorter than him. If it is indeed a difference in temperament that makes for the well-matched pair, then they were it. If Des had a somewhat anxious, occasionally gloomy disposition, Jan was there to sustain him with her pretty blonde looks, an irrepressible zest for life, and a large measure of down-to-earth common sense. Together they were fitting out an exceptionally good-looking concrete hull to the best standards in the yard. Des's work was painstaking, meticulous; he was the craftsman and we all admired his work.

If we were, as people are, varied in looks, temperament and build, we were nevertheless bound together by one obsession common to all – boats and the building of them.

As for Ken himself? He was the problem solver, the yard's engineering advisor. Everyone acknowledged his extraordinary repertoire of skills. At last, Ken was among his peers where he could earn the admiration and respect that he deserved. He stood more upright. I saw it. It was delicious justice. The man labelled 'handyman' was no more. No one would ever say to him again, 'Good old Ken … what a clever chap you are.' Patronising words when only one of you has oil up to your armpits. A pat on the back can come very close to being a gesture of contempt. The car won't start? Don't worry, Ken will fix it. And he invariably did. Another pat on the back, not even a drink or a mention of payment and Ken would never compromise his pride by asking.

I'd always seen it differently. Here was first choice for male companion on a desert island. He would identify all the raw materials and fashion shelter. He would make all the utensils we might need, probably even a primitive hand-cranked washing machine. Then he would capture food … all before the sun set on the first day.

'You're my hero,' I would tell him. And you could tell that he had never been called that before.

Sometimes the weather beat us all. I shall never forget one particular day when we set out to brave minus five degrees plus a wind chill factor that made it another ten degrees below that. Welding gloves and wellington boots froze to the steel wherever they touched. In steadily accelerating misery we played out one of the oldest games of all:

He: 'I can't very well give up before she does, can I? If I give in she will think less of me.'

She: 'If he really loved me he would notice that all my capillaries have disappeared. But, if I give up before he does he may think less of me.'

It still makes us blush with shame. Finally, after four hours of this stupidity we stared at each other in abject distress. We called it a day. It cured us of martyrdom. I cried with relief.

There was justice in the fact that we made no capital from the event though we did try it on. We had a self-righteous go at all the absentees who promptly declared that they expected nothing less from such a pair of fools. It was always like that. Ground base honesty. No quarter given, none asked for. Bloody nicks from chisel blades, blackened thumbs, welding burns, falls from ladders – all greeted with the utmost merriment. I had joined the environment of men at work. They were splendid times.

Chapter 7

The welding continued throughout that dreadful winter. Day after day, long into the afternoon darkness. The night frost would creep along the ground to suck the blood from our feet. Spring was late in coming. I began to suspect a conspiracy.

'Will you marry me, then?' Ken had kneeled in front of the chair where I was sitting cradling a mug of cocoa, wincing, almost crying, as the warmth defrosted my fingers.

'Married?' I said stupidly. I just couldn't think. At that moment, married just meant bloody cold.

The words stumbled and fell over themselves. 'Not now, Ken ... I love you, it's not that ... I'm sure you know ... let me think ... please ask me again... please ask ... but not now.'

Right, girl! You've caught up with your boulder – now what? Are you going to leave it where it is, mark the spot in case you want to find it again? Look around this strange landscape; what do you think of it? Want to stay here? If not, girl, what is it you want? You're an imago now, you can choose. Imagine not having any conventional framework to compare your life with, go on, imagine it: no oughts, no shoulds, no buts, no propers or corrects. It would mean sacrificing that carefully constructed compromise of yours, though.

I brought a hazel twig home, placed it into a jam jar of water and waited for it to become catkins and spring. And then I decided. What made the decision right was so simple in the end: It did not matter! If the nest I was about to build was ruined for any reason, at any time in the future, I'd build it again. I gave the boulder a shove, got it on the move again, and followed it. I had never felt so free, so self-determining or so unafraid. No one could make things matter: not Ken, not the boat, nor even the expectations of society – only I could make things matter. I waited to see whether he would ask again.

Meanwhile, Ken had been asked to weld some bracing straps to the keel of a boat that was lying in a yard at Isleworth. He had readily agreed. These modest sources of income were our lifeline.

Although officially it was the first day of spring, the early morning air was cold and crisp so we had wrapped up well in woollies and balaclava scarves.

A small huddle of men stood around waiting for the day's work to start. When the foreman arrived they began to shuffle. He was a good deal shorter than the men who stood their distance from him, but there was no doubt that he was the boss man. The men stayed silent, no one greeted him. Grim and silent, he stood watching us. The thin features of his face were fixed in a look of sour disapproval. The sort of man you could never think of as having once been a baby. His bird thin legs appeared to start from his shoulders.

I was struggling with the cables. The overnight frost had made them stiff and unwieldy. Having been warned that a long run would be needed to reach the power supply, we had extended our leads to twelve metres. I was doing my best to untangle these awkward lengths while Ken hauled the arc welder to the job.

For a moment we were startled. The A frame had spoken! 'You want to tell that lad to get on with it!'

Quick witted is Ken. 'Yes, she is a bit on the slow side.'

'She!?'

'Yes – my wife.'

We know he disappeared because we didn't see him again, though when or how quickly was a mystery. But then again, Ken is a big man and there is something about a full beard that disguises a man's intentions until the last minute. You could get a bloody nose just standing there wondering about intentions.

But he was still watching – we could feel it. That clear patch on the window of the portacabin office where the frost had been rubbed away kind of gave him away...

We reacted to this like a pair of naughty youngsters. Ken set up the gear, cut the strips of metal to size with the angle grinder, then, with a private wink, he handed me the welding helmet.

One should never pause at such moments. I took the helmet coolly enough I think, then proceeded to show off outrageously while Ken stood around with the men, and the hawk peered from his unseen perch. At least we fervently hoped he did since the whole staged performance was entirely for his benefit.

The arc rod went into its holder with a flamboyant twist of the wrist, spare rods dropped into hip pocket like a quiver full of arrows. A few 'expert' words to Ken about the correct amperage (which he had already set as usual though he duly pretended to twiddle the knobs). The final flourish was an Oscar-winning touch. I stroked the helmet over my face with a sweep of my elbow. This was something I had seen the old hands do but had never before tried for myself.

During the whole of the journey back we giggled and chuckled together like a pair of jubilant piglets who have just outwitted the Big Bad Wolf. Opportunities like that are not sent to be wasted.

'Did you hear what I called you?' Ken asked.

I smiled. 'Yes, I did.'

'Is that a yes?'

I gave him a yes look and we decided that May was a good month to be married.

Nothing changed about our days except that I now shared his commitment to the boat and to the style of life it would entail.

I hadn't realised that the hull must be joined up inside as well as out, short runs of weld every few inches to secure the plating to the honeycomb of ribs. Ken started in the stem. I started in the bow. One day, a few weeks later, we hoped to meet in the middle. Apart from the sacred lunch break, we hardly saw each other from daybreak to sundown. It was head down and persevere time without adding in any way to the boat's appearance. Tedious beyond belief and only marginally less boring than knitting a boat cover for an ocean liner.

From the outside it looked as though we had abandoned her. The only evidence of life, if you were standing close enough, was a muffled hiss, an occasional splutter. Inside the hull was a latticework of glinting lines as if an invasion of slugs had left their shiny tracks behind.

Consolidation, this is called. A very important aspect of the project. It must never be left to do another day because that day never comes. It is a point at which many amateur efforts come to a halt.

It was time to look for portholes, which was the same as saying that it was time to look at a few realities, money for one. The big one actually, since we had no money at all other than from the small jobs Ken took on from time to time. Brass portholes are expensive, even second-hand ones, and the chances of finding 15 of the same size and design in a scrapyard was as remote as raising £800 to buy them.

As so often happens when working in a boat-yard alongside like-minded people, the answer was close to hand. We had walked past our windows every day for a year. They were lying under Chris's boat. Half inch thick ovals made of perspex. His last post had been with British Airways and these were the windows from a Boeing 707 – oblong, with a slightly convex curve to them and having a very high fracture tolerance. They are replaced in aircraft regularly. Usually the old ones were scrapped but Chris thought they might come in handy for something. They did, they were meant for us all along, and from what more illustrious source than an airliner?

After flame cutting our apertures to fit them, we set up a mini production line to make the flanges for them. Ken was in his element. He enjoyed the engineer's challenge of giving discarded objects some purpose again, or better still, some entirely different application. It was the same with engines. Provided they still had all the necessary bits, no matter how ancient or ill-used, they must be coaxed back to life.

It was a strange preoccupation to witness. Whether it was just an idea or an immediate practical problem, it must first be battered around to the point of feeble-mindedness. The greater the challenge or the frustration, the more imaginative and complex the cursing. At the end of all this suffering he would enjoy a mysterious rapture of total satisfaction. I watched this ritual many times and always in complete confusion. After my first visit to an industrial scrapyard I came to understand some of it. Never all of it.

We fitted the first two windows with great excitement. Since they looked so much like eyes we drew brows, nose and tooth-laden mouth using welding chalk. The ugly portrait did little to flatter the boat but it was great fun for us. Fitting the other 13 became one of the tasks of ... 'consolidation', we muttered to each other.

We always had need of a stockpile of steel to manufacture into this or that. It was the main motive for our many trips to scrapyards. The secondary motive was more in the nature of a day out to the seaside. These excursions became a perfect antidote to our otherwise disciplined and punishing work schedule.

Although we were to range the length and breadth of the Thames Valley, the most familiar was our local yard. The gaffer there took a shine to me and I to him. He often put items by that he thought we could use. He would listen carefully and knowingly as we described our progress with the boat. As soon as we appeared at the gates he would climb out of the tipper lorry, or we might see his approach in the distance, tightrope walking across a girder or leaping from one engine block to another, as if they were pebbles in a stream. It was surprising that someone so large could be so nimble. His greeting was always indirect.

'I see you're still keeping him at it!' Or he might say, 'Here they are again, what are they on the scrounge for this time?'

I was astonished by the scrapyards. In one corner, a house-high pile of aluminium swarf, glinting like tinsel, shooting bright sunlight in every direction. In another, ton on ton of penny-sized stampings – rubbish from some industrial process and now piled here like treasure trove. It was here that I noticed a smell to steel. Subtle yet distinct. Steel burning, steel rusting, new steel.

Ken was in his element and soon enough so was I. What could we make of this? What could we make of that? We always carried a small magnet with us. It was tossed backwards and forwards so that we could each distinguish between mild and stainless steel. A third of the boat was built from the trophies we found in these industrial graveyards: mast supports, angle iron for the bunks, bulkhead bracing, housing tube for the propeller shaft, and no less than two thirds of the ballast. Many hundreds of pounds saved, many marvellous days out.

Ron, the gaffer, would be there at the gates to total up the scrap weight of whatever we carried in our arms or dragged along behind us. He invariably discounted my puny armful from the calculations as being too trifling to take into account.

As with his greeting, so with his farewell.

'You keep him at it now. You're the boss!' At which signal I would nudge Ken in the back until he executed an exaggerated stumble, then look back for Ron's nod of approval, his hug of affection – a really nice man.

Now it really isn't easy to earn the dubious honour of being banned from a scrapyard. Ken swears to this day that he was blameless. It was a small unlikely looking yard but it turned out to be a gold-mine in our scheme of things – or rather, it should have been. Three tons of solid steel bar for the ballast at only £50 a ton. We never did the deal. The crane driver underestimated the load he was swinging towards the waiting skip – it sank excruciatingly slowly through the cab of an adjacent truck. It cost the proprietor a bomb. Ken was given a red card, banned on the spot – for life. Not because it was his fault in any way, but some people are said to be jinxes. That's what he kept shouting, 'Jinx ... bloody jinx!' The yard governor had decided Ken was one of them.

The finest yard of all is in Southampton. Acres of dismembered ships and submarines. Engines so large you can practically walk around inside their carburettors. Everything on a colossal scale: ropes and hawsers as thick as anacondas, house-sized anchors, flea-sized people.

When we returned to our 'ship' she looked small as a dinghy – but not for long...

Chapter 8

What a memorable day! What a heart-of-the-matter, fateful, consequential, outstanding, meaningful sort of day! A day to spur you on, the kind of day that tells you, flat out straight, that you are gazing in the right direction.

It started innocuously enough. We were sitting in a small transport cafe in Chertsey where we treated ourselves once a week to a bacon and eggs breakfast. The front faced onto the high street, which was how we came to notice the scrap lorry passing by. Written on the cab was a name we didn't recognise from our usual haunts. We quickly exchanged looks, swallowed down a last huge mouthful, grabbed what was left of the toast, paid the bill with money on the table, and rushed out to follow it.

The prospect of a hitherto unknown yard made us feel quite light-headed – that familiar tingle of expectancy. We rarely left a yard without some item that would serve the project. Fortunately it was still rush hour and so we were able to catch up with the vehicle and follow it.

Ken had long been keeping an eye open for the second axle from which to make up the trolley for the launch. He had already acquired the rear axle from an old bomb trailer that he had decided would be tough enough for the job. Now he was after the monster from an eight-wheeler truck to serve as the front steerable axle.

OK, so it may seem implausible, but as we drove into the yard, there, – not 50 yards from us – was a man using heavy cutting gear. The oxyacetylene torch was still alight. He stooped again to prepare ... yes! ... the front steerable axle from an eight-wheeler. He was cutting it into log-sized pieces ready for transporting to the reprocessing plant. He had barely scored the surface of the steel before we were at his side, pleading with him to stop. We had to shake his arm and shout above the general hubbub of the yard. I think he was a bit frightened by us ganging up on him like that, but eventually he seemed to realise that we wanted no more than a stay of execution.

After assuring him that we would be back, we located the shed that served as office and tea cabin and shuffled a way through the men and the yellow fog. By then I was quite accustomed to the fog. It's a potent mixture of tobacco smoke and body odours in which deals are struck and where notes are peeled from thick wads of money.

We were strangers. The man sitting at the table fixed us with a suspicious stare. We asked him how much he wanted for the precious axle. Ten pounds. A fair price, but we had been paid for the Isleworth job with a cheque and I realised, with dismay, that we didn't have quite that much cash with us. That we possessed any cash at all was simply another act of providence. It was perfectly obvious – we were meant to have that axle.

We therefore placed our trust in the parable of the five loaves and the two fishes and proceeded to turn our pockets out onto the gaffer's table. After hastily retrieving washers, half used welding rods, brown-white handkerchiefs and lumps of slag, the grand total came to £7.92. I saw Ken's face drop. I stepped forward in front of the gaffer and stood there respectfully. Doing things on Ken's behalf tended to fill me with a sight more courage than the negligible amount I had inherited. I looked the gaffer straight in the eye. With acute embarrassment mixed with heartfelt appeal, I asked him:

'Would that be enough?'

He threw his head back in surprise, or heaven help me, was it outrage? I stepped back in fright, bumping into the men who stood behind me. I now suspect that either he hadn't really noticed me before or he suddenly realised I was a woman. Either way, he carefully studied me up and down while picking up the scattered coins one by one. It took an age. The hut was stilled now. Silent and tense as a saloon bar in the Wild West before the shoot out. My left leg started to give me trouble. I thought he might hear it knocking against the edge of his table.

Finally he spoke in a lilting Irish accent: 'Will yer look at that now – poor little blighter.'

Nor did it sound in the least like an insult. Looking like a blighter was easy: I would have tried to look like a fish in oil if I thought that was what he wanted!

'I don't know how you do it.' Ken was driving along in high spirits, the precious axle stowed behind his seat. I imitated the seductive voice in a washing powder commercial. 'You too can have size four boots and baggy boilers.'

Providence at work again. It was dozens of adventures like these that gave character to our endeavour and energised our days. The axles would have to wait three more years before they played their particularly illustrious, if short-lived, part in the proceedings.

I never grasped the knowledge of the whole. Ken held the complete jigsaw in his head. His research into the how and the means, the materials and costing, the fabricating and adapting, was every bit as exacting as any of the physical labour. His mind would often become soggy with fretting and worrying. There was no one to share that part of the load. The moment one problem was solved, the next loomed. Building a yacht from scratch on a shoestring budget would create a thousand of them.

On the 7 May 1982, we finally joined our safety lines together. Ken's grieving was over. Losing Helen had added another patch of the scar tissue we all carry around our hearts but he was whole again so we married each other. Nothing changed, which showed that it was the right thing to do. I bought a new blouse and borrowed a skirt. After a small lunch gathering at the cricket club, the wedding party went out to the crease and played two celebration overs. The bride's team won prettily. Richard's wife, Jenny, made us a wonderful wedding cake and no one worried about where they should sit at the table.

I moved permanently into the caravan, feeling sad to leave my beloved river behind but content to be patient until we could return again in the craft of Ken's making. It was the first time I had been landlocked for 14 years – at least it wasn't a house. I didn't want a house. Fortunately the club grounds were situated in the suburbs of Egham so there were still a few birds to enjoy and trees to admire.

We called it the 'line camp'. Although it was a comfortable enough habitation, we were always planning to live on the boat permanently so we made no fuss about the niceties that usually embellish a home. I must also admit that I shared the discomfort most women have about the 'presence' of another female who had lived, loved, cooked and washed the dishes there. I kept the inside as reasonably tidy as anyone can who chooses to live with an amateur boat-builder, which is not a standard acceptable to most mothers, but the outside looked exactly like a gypsy encampment. It couldn't be helped – we had to store our materials somewhere. We had long ago used up our allotted space at the boat-yard. There is no way that a pile of scrap metal can be persuaded to look tidy. Even the pedestal urns that once prettied the doorway were eventually ousted to make room for an air compressor, collections of softwood, and a miscellany of iron tubes and engine parts.

My 'honeymoon' was spent making the water and diesel tanks; a task that finally earned me my full welder's 'wings'. Ken drew up the dimensions and marked up the steel plate. I then gas cut the sections before carefully welding them up inside and out. We fixed two baffle plates in each tank to counteract water turbulence in heavy seas.

Ken got on with some specialist jobs: setting up the rudder fixings, propeller tube, the engine shaft, all in preparation for the ballasting. It took me about three weeks of continuous work to complete all six tanks and their inspection plates at a fraction of the cost of stainless steel versions. They had been designed very carefully to fit the contours of the hull, giving maximum capacity to space. Having done away with two of the nine berths suggested in the plans, we could now carry sufficient fuel and water for genuine long-distance sailing. It would give us great confidence if things went wrong, said Ken.

'One hundred and eighty gallons of each. We could flop about out there for a good two months with that much fuel and water.'

'Flop about?' I said faintly, 'out there?' It was the first time I had spared a thought for that bit.

The three water tanks were pressure tested to 10 psi before being sent off to be galvanised. These one-off jobs gave us a feeling of acceleration and real progress. Just as well. It helped us to confront the fact that four more jobs had to be faced, each one as daunting as the hull welding had been.

'I suppose it's time you met my mum,' Ken said one day.

'But you've never mentioned her before, love.'

'I don't see a lot of her, she can be quite difficult, you mustn't mind what she says sometimes.' And that was all he was prepared to say.

The saying goes: if you want to find out what your prospective wife/husband will be like go and meet the mother. Sometimes true, sometimes entirely false. Either way, mothers are powerful and must be met. We decided to go the following weekend...

Chapter 9

A small, round, brown-haired, dark-eyed woman opened her door to us, and uttered her first words to the son she had not seen for nearly two years...

'Ugh! Look at you, that horrible beard ... shave it off ... dirty, it looks dirty, Kenny.'

A perfunctory hug before turning back into the room, leaving Ken to shut the door. On me! A few yards in, she swivelled her head barely a quarter way round. 'You'd better bring the girl in.'

'I divorce thee,' I muttered as I followed him into the living-room.

This then was Beatrice Gogay, mother to Ken and four other big lusty children. The shaper of his eyes, of his head of hair, his size 13 feet, and of his volatile, restless, angry temperament. I must not panic!

Her use of the diminutive 'Kenny' grated. I sat down dutifully though without being invited to and watched her effect on him. He changed to suit her: changed into short trousers; his feet didn't seem to touch the floor any longer; he fidgeted in his chair, was watchful of her in the way of kids who are ready to duck if need be. It dawned on me then – he was afraid of her. I had a nasty flashback to the caterpillar years, quickly controlled it by calmly imagining my hands around her throat, inwardly smiling at how remote such a prospect had become.

For many years I had benefited from having a psychiatrist as friend and mentor. At a rate of, say, one psychological text book a month, I had read some 200 tomes and treatises. But what I was witnessing now seemed entirely new and different. I'm out of my depth here by hundreds of metres, I thought, ruefully. This took both the biscuit and every other cake on the plate!

It was impossible to relate to her. She was a woman without a single social grace. The place she inhabited was a field of tightly tied straw bundles, each one of them a resentment or a bitterness. No one cared about her, no one visited, the food they brought her to eat was rotten, her daughter was horrible to her: quick, poking comments. These were dreadful lies because I knew that two of her children lived within walking distance. Between them they called in every single day. As she spoke, her face screwed up into an ugly mask of terrible rage and she would spit out her invectives, saliva and all. A second later some private thought would intrude and cause her to giggle. There seemed nothing to grasp, nothing to make any rounded sense of her. This was a lot more than just the rantings of a fractious old woman and a lot less than plain mad.

She totally ignored me.

Not once did she ask about the boat, nor did she seem to care anything about Ken's personal welfare or happiness, or even acknowledge the fact that we were man and wife. Ken was ignoring me, too, as if afraid to lead me into trouble. I was parched, dying for a cup of tea, knew that such a normal gesture of hospitality would not be forthcoming. It was totally bizarre.

Distanced as I was from the encounter, there was time to look around the room. I would have done so anyway but this time there was precious else to do. Clues there must be, somewhere in this room – there always were. When entering a house for professional reasons I had always looked for them: animals that rushed away to hide, children who kept a precisely determined distance from their parents as if joined to them by a string of critical length: arm's length. A too-tidy house, a sterile, unlived-in house, or a vibrant, moderately dishevelled, stimulating house.

And clues there were. They jostled and nudged, were wedged together and overflowing, taking up every available horizontal space in the room – photographs of her children (dozens of them), dusty and yellowed from years of standing in their same allotted space. The same children who had once plotted together about how to throw her from the top of the stairs to the bottom, who had begged their father to divorce her, who still feared her. Two of them openly loathed her. Only Ken and his sister Fay persevered, still looking for some token of approval that would never come.

I wondered what had caused this otherwise intelligent woman to be the way she was. Her quixotic sense of humour was especially confusing. There was something manic and sarcastic about it, like laughing with a clenched fist. At the world? I had to know. It was important that I should know. This was about Ken's caterpillar years and having a mother like Beatrice made me wonder whether I could live with Ken: with his rages, his frustrations, his restless search for approval. The boat he was building carried more significance than ever – he could *not* fail.

Some days later, after we had recovered from the visit, I asked him to tell me stories about his mother. And one of them said all there was to say ... about sorrow.

When Ken's father went to war in 1939, Beatrice was left with four young children to raise. Theirs had been a lusty union, the births came in regular succession: three boys and a girl. Left to shoulder the responsibilities alone, she applied herself with an energy and possessiveness that would overcome any obstacle that dared oppose her. She was described as a 'difficult' woman even then, telling other women flat out that they were ugly, or fat, or that she didn't like their dresses. But for her children she was the story-book mother, one who read fireside stories to them as they lay heaped up on the floor beside her chair, who could somehow find the wartime butter and eggs and tinned jam when no one else could, who taught them all to sew, and iron and cook. She did it first in London until the days of the Blitz when children were ordered to be evacuated. She then found them all a house in Oxfordshire after aggressively refusing to be separated from the children. The Oxfordshire countryside was an idyllic place for kids who had only known the East End of London. It did for Ken exactly what Worcestershire had done for me.

'When your father comes home...' When your father comes home ... wartime slogan. Wartime fantasy. Gaining in strength with the passing years. 'Things will be better' ... 'things will be easier.'

Benjamin Gogay did not come home for nearly seven years. He served throughout the African Campaign, first under the command of Alanbrooke, then Montgomery. He stayed with the Eighth Army while it suffered in Egypt, stayed with it for the whole bloodying struggle through Italy, then finally into Germany and victory. He only ever told one story about his experiences, the time his convoy was strafed from the air, when he baled out from his vehicle. Many of his comrades died that day. When he returned to look at the damage, he saw that his seat had been shot into shreds. He had lived. His friends had died. Such were the livid and vivid moments in the war that changed men and would never let them go. These were what the nightmares and the crying would be about.

He bought the handbag in Egypt, made from camel leather, beautifully tooled and shaped. He thought she would like it. He carried it with him throughout the rest of his war, carefully wrapped and placed in the middle of his knapsack with the soft items: socks and spare vests. He lay over it in foxholes, wrapped it again in canvas to protect it from the rain.

The war finally ended. It was Ken who noticed the khaki-clad figure walking the village road towards their house. He ran to tell his mother.

'What have you brought me ... where is it? ... Where's the gold?' Benjamin carefully unwrapped his memory of her, precious to him as a photograph in a wallet, and gave it to her.

She threw it to one side, and continued to rummage frantically in his knapsack. She had heard about it from other women. Men had brought back looted gold, watches from the wrists of dead men, precious things, money things.

That was when the next war started. Their war. And it was just as bloody and unforgiving. Attrition and blame. Dashed hopes on both sides.

None of the children could remember a peaceful day after that. There must have been: another child was born. But the atmosphere was raw and wounding and in the exchanges of fire between the parents every child was hit by a bullet.

Benjamin was an unassuming, quiet man. He managed this new war by working long hours. He established a window-cleaning business, earned good money at it, spent the rest of his loveless hours tending his garden or cycling for miles on his bicycle. He was rarely home.

Beatrice became more and more outrageous in her behaviour. The contradictions were the most damaging. In favour, out of favour, a slap, a hug, five minutes apart and no reason to it. Always too quick to adjust to or anticipate, too arbitrary to fabricate strategies that might placate her. She spent her generous weekly allowance in spitefully wasteful ways. Demanded more, insulted his trade, complained that if she had married someone else she might have become a 'lady'.

He had fought a war and won and still lost. She, literate, ambitious and socially aspiring, saw all her hopes evaporate. He responded by becoming a pacifist while Beatrice took up arms.

The war. All over the country there were disappointed men and women who didn't understand each other any more, who couldn't grasp how each had prevailed or the fact that both of them had been to war.

Damn that tragic, distorted, war-torn, war-caused scenario.

I understood Ken's rages better now. It was the legacy inflicted on each of them. They all raged. Angry about it all … just as I had been.

Ken would never buy me a gift or remember my birthday. Of course not – I might disapprove of what he had chosen. He would never celebrate a holiday. He dreaded Christmases. Of course he did – they had become the stuff of nightmares in his house. If I had not discovered the source, I would have thought he didn't care, wouldn't I?

But I had been loved … it had worked. I loved Ken … it would work.

Chapter 10

We didn't speak much about his mother after that. Nor did we visit very often. There was only one worthwhile statement for us to make about it all and that was to build an imago.

Above all else, Ken is a mechanic. The engine and power supplies were his special preserve. It took two years to track down the engine he would finally be satisfied with. At one stage he had four lumps (as engine people call them) at the caravan. All were worked on and made to run but each was found lacking for some reason or other.

Richard rang us one afternoon. He had heard of a promising second-hand engine in Lancaster, a fully marinised 3.6 litre Ford. Since it was a later model than the one we had acquired from a tractor, there seemed a good chance that Ken might cannibalise the two and produce one good engine.

We looked at each other. Did it feel like another omen? Was this the one? Ten minutes to throw a couple of sleeping bags into our battered diesel truck and off to test providence again. Off on the most appalling journey we have ever undertaken, including those at sea.

It was somewhere in deepest Lancashire. One hundred and fifty miles at a top speed of 40 mph, in a vehicle that can only be called comfortable if you compare it with a fairground horror ride.

Our 'there and then' decision was made at 6pm. The plan was to drive to the outskirts of the city, sleep overnight and try to find the address in the early morning when there would be less traffic about. Hopefully that would leave us with plenty of time for a slow drive back, maybe with our engine in the back.

Another bout of childish excitement caused us to overlook the obvious – it was eight degrees below freezing at midnight. By two o'clock in the morning, when we finally chugged into Lancaster, it was a full twelve below.

I fervently hope to God that we never endure another night like it. Even with all our clothes on, the two sleeping bags, and me lying on top of Ken, we shivered uncontrollably.

Sometime during that dreadful night, I felt a familiar urge to wee or bust. I found myself debating the issue. Wouldn't I really rather bust? Consideration for my partner and friend took the decision in a very close vote.

I clambered out, stiff with suffering. We had driven into an empty car-park to spend the night. Several street lights lined the perimeter, giving the expanse of concrete the look of an arena. Having completed what felt like a very public performance, and, in fear lest an icicle should form, I scrambled back into the tiny sleeping compartment behind the seats. I could hear Ken moaning quietly. Whether we actually slept or finally slipped into a shallow coma, we neither knew nor cared. Either way, we surfaced or regained consciousness at 7am, stiff as coat-hangers. Etched in the frost layer was a tell-tale rivulet glinting yellow in the bleary sunlight.

Such is the robustness of the human spirit in general, and of boat-builders in particular, that three mugs of tea and a cafe breakfast later, we were restored. Just another campaign memory after all. You can get quite smug about suffering.

As if to justify our ordeal, the engine was judged to be suitable. It was right from the moment Ken saw it. Ten minutes after unloading it back at the caravan he was stripping it down.

The lump itself cost £250. Another £100 to replace the cylinder linings and pistons and to have the crankshaft reground. Valves and springs were replaced during the overhaul. Ken lavished all his expertise on this, the heart of his vessel. He made it a thing of beauty. The stainless steel water-jacketed exhaust system and the heat exchanger were all handmade in the shed at the caravan. In our local scrapyard we found several metres of the high pressure steam pipe work that a well-known sweet-making factory used for pumping chocolate. As well as looking pristine in the engine room, it also reduced the amount of expensive pressure hosing we would otherwise have needed.

One of these pipes was still full of solidified chocolate. It resisted all efforts to clear it. We tried scraping it out, ramming it out, boiling it out, but it seemed that nothing would shift it. We left it outside. The answer would come. Ken would ruminate.

A week later we noticed that the chocolate had disappeared as far as the first bend. When we shone a torch inside we could see what looked like teeth marks! Very perplexing. We took turns at a nature watch. Our obliging tube cleaners turned out to be a pair of squirrels who clearly found chocolate as irresistible as the rest of the population. They chewed away with greedy enthusiasm and eventually popped out through the other side. Job done!

The largest bill we faced throughout the project was £600 for the bell housing and gearbox. As usual, Ken had tracked down a second-hand version but it was simply too large. Modem gearboxes are so compact that the space we gained was felt to outweigh the extra cost. Nevertheless, it was a difficult decision that involved more than the money. The older version was Ken's sort of machinery – simple replaceable working parts inside an explosion-resistant box. Solid! Fortunately we had just enough money left over from the sale of the houseboat to cover it.

'Don't break your leg now, love, because I haven't the money to dial for an ambulance.' Penniless again. We laughed. I don't know why we laughed, but we did.

If the standard of finish inside the boat is a matter of particular pride to me, then so is the propulsion system to Ken. It represented months and months of highly skilled work. I am not qualified to describe the full scope of his effort, but Richard, our reliable sceptic, said it was good, so it really was very good. Much of what he fabricated for the engine room had been manufactured a full two years before it was assembled into the system.

'I've got something to show you,' Ken said one day. He unveiled it from under a grimy tarpaulin. It was the rudder. An immensely strong, handsome looking rudder, red leaded and ready for painting. He must have made it weeks before the keel was laid. Not, I suspected, just because it was a nice finished item to have tucked away – there had to have been something symbolic about it, too.

Chapter 11

Some of the work was fun, a lot of it was tedious, most of it was hard. Occasionally, it was brutal...

The task was simple enough in theory. Deposit seven tons of iron ballast into the 23 keel boxings and bed it all in with concrete, adding a proprietary water proofer to reduce porosity. Utterly straightforward!

All the material that had been painstakingly collected over the previous three years was lying in two huge mounds under the hull. Surely that much would fill the boat to the water-line? Nearly every lump of it was representative of the enormous goodwill that is generated once you admit you are building a boat. We were never once refused permission to glean from industrial skips after we had described our purpose, and many an amiable chat was to be enjoyed in the process. There must be many who have since wondered whether anything came of it all.

As always, our methods were governed by the obligation to accept labour over cost but there was a satisfaction to be gained from that, too. Lead is undoubtedly the best and most convenient material to use, but the talk was of hundreds of pounds. Luckily we were able to keep the tally down to £200 plus some overdeveloped muscles and six weeks of backache.

There was every conceivable shape in the engineering repertoire: hexagon bar, round bar, flat bar, rings, rounds and any amount of random shaped offcuts. The problem of reorganising them into a dense mass was a mathematician's delight, or a Rubik nightmare – in my case it was the latter. I had read somewhere that it was all to do with the design of your brain but thought it best not to go into that aspect because whatever it was I didn't have it.

Learning that you may have a defective brain isn't a confidence booster.

'It would be interesting to find out about that,' said Ken.

My reply was a bit short. 'I don't do brains.'

Ken appeared to view the possibilities with some relish but generously decided that I could 'play at it'.

'You'll enjoy it,' he said.

I'm not sure to this day whether it was true benevolence on his part or downright deceit. Then again, he did have a shot-blaster to design and make so it was incumbent on me to try, at least.

There were dozens of possible combinations in both vertical and horizontal planes. Oh well, advanced matrices would be a doddle after this. The tireless old arm saw came into its own again, gnawing its way through inch-thick flat bar and five-inch rounds without too much complaint other than a chronic dependence on a regular slug or two of grease. We could not have built the boat without that indefatigable piece of machinery. It was our pit pony. At the end of its usefulness we found it a good home where it was only used occasionally. Semi-retirement seemed the right and proper acknowledgement of its sterling service.

Having measured the cubic capacity of each section of keel boxing, we reproduced the mass required by first laying it up on the ground. It was then possible to work out what weight we could expect if the section was filled to maximum theoretical capacity: a simple maths formula based on the fact that one cubic foot of steel weighs 558 pounds. Our goal was 90 per cent or better and we generally managed that, sometimes up to 95 per cent. The bathroom scales were sacrificed to the cause. Every last piece was weighed and written up on a blackboard before being laid in.

This was the easy part, you only got a headache from that. The hard part was carrying the ballast into the boat. Ken could carry 60 pounds at a time – up the ladder, across the cockpit, down the companionway steps, into the bilges. I graduated very slowly from 15 pounds to 30. My legs have never been quite the same since.

For six weeks it was a criminal offence for anyone to climb the ladder without ballast in their hands. Even our friends were handed a ticket to board that weighed five or ten pounds. We each took our fair share in mixing concrete and carrying up the sloppy mess in buckets.

To eliminate any air spaces, each layer of steel was rammed home with scaffold poles until the concrete oozed out. It was grim, humourless toil with day-dreams and fantasies to match: penal servitude in the quarries, pounding rice in the tropics. Feeble attempts at boosting each other's morale tended to be rather short lived: 'gung-ho' rhythms usually; truncated bits of song. Nothing very imaginative.

'You load sixteen tons...' Thump!

'The grand old Duke of York...' Thump! 'He had ten thousand men...' Thump!

But the songs petered out. We each turned inside ourselves where we could deal with the torment in our own ways.

Even with such precise packing there remained the odd cubic inch of space in each compartment. We filled these with a dense mixture made up of penny-sized iron stampings, similar to the pile we had seen at the scrapyard. As a thickly impregnated slurry it was ideal.

As we pounded in this last layer, the concrete stopped oozing and started spitting instead. For some reason this behaviour irritated me beyond endurance. The concrete was doing it deliberately – just to be spiteful! Our nerve endings were already raw from fatigue so a couple of teeny weeny ventings, a mild objection or two were inevitable. Surely! When the lid came off, however, it got ugly! An hysterical outburst, actually. And isn't it interesting how you can hold a hell of a lot back until someone is fool enough to 'say' something?

A glob of concrete hit me in the eye. I swore with real venom.

'A perfect parabolic trajectory,' mused Ken.

'Clever bastard!' I yelled.

For the rest of that day, as well as sulking, I was consumed with one solitary life goal: I must, first person imperative, get a glob of concrete up Ken's nostril before I died.

We never wanted to be that tired again yet knew we would be. At least we discovered the second of two good reasons for hugging someone. We added solace to affection. As a spontaneous outlet for our affection we probably hug each other as many times a day as most folk drink cups of tea. We've hugged on building sites, in scrapyards and 20 feet up in a fork-lift.

Ken realised that I had reached the current limits of my physical endurance – I would become more robust as time went on. He dropped his own scaffold pole, took mine gently from my hands and enveloped me in his big frame (you don't have to be big – anyone can do it). It takes five minutes. It works.

When Ken was troubled I couldn't exactly 'envelope' him, but I could get both arms around his shoulders, press his head into my belly and hold on tight. I suppose that in some situations we may have caused consternation, even embarrassment, but in the boat-yard they were content with calling us the 'budgies'.

Our boat was built with these hugs. It was a way of dealing with today's limits, never yesterday's or tomorrow's.

The last day of the ballasting seemed to grab us both by the throat. We had acquired a lump of steel that fitted one of the keel boxes almost exactly. We had saved it for the last effort, since it weighed almost two hundredweight. A block and tackle was set up so that it could be hauled up and swung into the boat through the cockpit floor. This area would be welded in last after the engine and tanks had been installed.

I've always suffered from directional dyslexia, particularly where left and right are concerned so it was inevitable that I would pull the wrong chain. Ken had very carefully taken up the tension in order to lift the steel a few inches from the ground. Just as carefully, I lowered it down again. I saw his face tighten. A stern voice suggested that I 'pull the other one'.

Those instructions (not to mention the way they were delivered) were just a little too obvious, even for my taste, since it was well within my intellectual capacity, even when dulled by tiredness, to realise that when there were only two chains if the first choice was wrong then the second would be right – or was it left?

By the time I had got through that torrent of thinking, I had let go of both chains so fate decreed that exactly the same thing would happen again. Ken duly tensioned the block off the ground. I duly lowered it down again.

He'll break soon, I thought. Ken remained silent but I could tell he wasn't quite himself. I did eventually happen on the right one and began to heave, as evenly and smoothly as I could so as not to swing or jar.

To be fair to Ken, I think he was more concerned about whether the small block could stand the strain for long. Anyway, he called up to me...

'You can pull quicker than that!'

I boiled over with rage. I practically incinerated myself.

'What are you trying to turn me into?' I yelled at him. 'A bloody gorilla?'

He laughed. Foolish man. I contemplated murder. A hug of very high quality was needed to sort that one out.

Much later, we were sitting together, separate in mind, cradling our mugs of tea, each staring at our own patch of ground. The ballast was in – all seven tons – by hand, in small lumps. What on earth were we about? Barely two furlongs of the mile and here we sat, hunched and drooping with exhaustion. Irritable as children.

Yet however tired we felt at the end of the day, the next morning we awoke with the urge to carry on. There was a simple explanation that had nothing to do with either incentive or masochism. You can slow down. You can sometimes potter about aimlessly for a day. You can even walk around in circles. What you dare not do is stop. When things are going well and the work is easy, yes, but when the labour is hard it is dangerously easy in the boat-building game for the pause to become a full stop.

Chapter 12

Ballasting? Merely an initiation test, a first-round trial of strength, a warm-up, a wearing in of new boots.

It left us feeling a bit light-headed. Here was proof that we could deal with tedium and fatigue. What we could never know, until the very end, was whether we could sustain the sheer volume of work: could we go on repeating the same degree of effort over and over again? Like the splendidly optimistic song, could we 'pick ourselves up', dust off the concrete, the welding grime, the paint, the oil, the polystyrene, and 'start all over again'?

After cracking open our boiler suits, they were disposed of by standing them next to the dustbins. We thought of saving them for a fancy dress ball but it was not the party season. First prize without a doubt: Ken as an altar candle, while I stood an excellent chance of second as a Hell's Angel in 'originals'.

Neither of us felt any resentment about particular tasks since by then we knew which of us was best suited to the job in hand. There were the same elements to each small part as in the project as a whole – planning, toolmaking, shaping up, consolidation and finishing. Ken made himself responsible for the first three phases and I for the last two. Fortunately it suited our temperaments to perfection. I need to finish jobs while Ken enjoys starting something new.

It was about this time that we shared an experience that would ultimately lead to the naming of the boat. We had given the subject a lot of thought. We wanted a name that would embrace the whole project, with a wealth of meaning to it. Whatever the choice, I would see Ken's name there, his *nom-de-plume*, because that is who she really is. Stalwart names like *Endeavour*, *Steadfast* or *Perseverance* sounded altogether too warrior-like for a peace-loving vessel. It must be a name that would celebrate her: something soft around the edges yet enduring. A strong, truthful name.

All work? No distractions? No smaller pleasures, treats or diversions? Of course there were. Lots of them, plenty of them, though none necessitated buying a ticket or checking out the wine label. We couldn't even afford a cinema outing.

We kept a fish tank in the caravan and tadpoles in the Butler sink outside. Both tank and sink were bought as a job lot at the same time as Ken picked up an old James motorcycle to renovate. Playthings to suit: Ken had something to tinker with and I could indulge my passion for pond life.

As soon as the tank was cleaned up and resealed, we set off for the local brook to find the stock for our jamjar aquarium. Early spring mornings still cold enough to make our noses run, the new grass saturated with dew, crane-flies scrambling away from our next footprint, tiaras glistening in the bushes, branches dripping liquid diamonds onto our heads. And we, with our seaside nets and peanut butter jars, feeling very young and carefree.

During the rest of our time at the caravan that fish tank, with its minnows, sticklebacks and small green tench, was a constant source of delight. Sometimes we would bring back 'visitors for the day' – newts, great diving beetles, water boatmen. We would watch them for a few hours then return them to their home pond.

Our favourite residents were the nymph and larval forms of various flying insects: caddis and dragonfly. It was a shared pleasure. I was so happy about that and really couldn't imagine any other man I knew coming out with me to catch tadpoles!

One morning I rushed out to the shed in consternation.

'Ken! One of the nymphs has hatched … I can't find the case and I can't find the dragonfly itself.'

'I'll come.'

We searched frantically for nearly an hour before we finally found it. The nymphal case was attached to the inside fold of the curtain and the dragonfly was in the corner of the ceiling. It enchanted us. The splendid creature was a full three and a half inches long. It had emerged from a nymph a quarter its size. An impossible birth. It hung there like a jewel-encrusted broach, shimmering with newness – a broach worthy of Helen of Troy, worthy of Cleopatra herself.

We climbed onto the sofa, muddy boots and all, so that we could gaze at the incredible translucent wings, delicate as tissue yet crisp and strong as Irish linen. Between the huge yellow eyes lay the small dome of its head. It was covered with a baby-fine down of delicate hairs. We wanted to stroke it there but feared harming it.

We found another nymph. This time we monitored it carefully. And we were there to see its clumsy exodus from water. After persuading it to fix onto a horse chestnut leaf, we waited.

I took the first watch. At two in the morning the thorax split open. I woke Ken quickly and together we watched and photographed as the dragonfly emerged, crumpled and pale. It had a ligament around it that acted like a safety harness against which it strained to withdraw its abdomen. It was so perfectly tensioned that it ruptured at the precise moment of extraction. Very gradually it began to swell up and take form. Slowly the colours appeared, then deepened and finally glowed.

To our way of thinking we had witnessed one of the most moving spectacles in nature. There is no art form from the hand of man to do it justice.

At dawn we noticed that the wings were beginning to quiver with a humming bird frequency. It was ready to fly. Ken took it outside perched on his forefinger. As he held it up to the early warmth of the sun the quivering became more urgent. Within a minute it was gone. We felt deeply moved and privileged. What touched us most was that such a glorious creature should emerge from something as nondescript as a dull brown nymph. It was more than a contradiction. It was one of those experiences where the truth is still impossible, even after you have seen it with your own eyes.

Two summers later. We were sitting together eating our sandwiches and gazing, first at each other, then at the boat. Our rusty hulk was totally transformed. The hull above the water-line and the whole of the superstructure gleamed with the first coat of grey primer. The paint had joined all the parts together into a 'whole' look. We saw the overall shape of our boat for the first time. A metamorphosis. Our first sight of her final form. We went out on that same day and filled in the registration forms. Her name is *Imago*.

Chapter 13

After the ballasting, I felt utterly drained and deeply discouraged. Female resentments added lumpy gravy to the miserable dish in front of me and spoiled my appetite.

Silent nagging: putting in the same hours, mister, plus a bit of overtime mister. You know: laundry, shopping, washing-up, picking up discarded socks, preparing for sex, and what's for dinner tonight?

'He expects too much of you.'

'He's never once said he loves me.'

'Are you going to stand for that?'

'I'm not sure,' I said miserably. Girl talk. Solidarity. Them and us. The war.

Failure and betrayal, too. Sitting with my sisters this way, running over to the female camps in kitchens and sitting-rooms, drinking cold coffee, eating sweet things for comfort. Cataloguing enemy atrocities, their patronising ways, bad sex, cool sex, ugly sex, slam dunk American sex (as one woman declared to hoots of sad laughter).

I knew that many women felt refreshed after such gatherings, needed them as regularly as a fix to vent their frustrations, even fury, or used them to seek either the courage to stay – or the courage to leave. No one ever discussed what contribution they, as women, might have made to the mess.

'Did you have a nice time, love?'

'Mmm ... er, yes, it was fun.' Hoping he didn't ask what we talked about. Feeling like an adulterous woman returning from an assignation, wishing I could have tiptoed in while he was asleep.

This was a serious assault on my belief system. I had to restore my faith: that a rewarding and compatible relationship with a man was possible. The pilot light flared and spluttered – fear again.

The evidence wasn't encouraging, the witnesses were credible. The prosecution case, convened in kitchens and sitting-rooms, sounded persuasive, damning. The defence case, convened in pubs and clubs, equally convincing. Enough to make a caterpillar's skin crawl: bad noises, quarrelling, recriminations, pushing, lip curling, harsh voices.

It must not happen to me – I'll die.

I didn't go down to the boat-yard for a couple of days, feigned not feeling very well, and wrote a fantasy dialogue to see where it would go ... to see whether I would stay.

Words spilled out of my head. Mature voices examined the subject – alien voices, lacking prejudice or personal agenda. Voices from the future. I had to get them down on paper, then, perhaps, I could quell the disquiet I felt inside me, sort things out. I would pretend I was a volunteer in a training programme, which, when completed, would make me the female delegate in a summit meeting between man and woman...

Chapter 14

Becoming empty was the hardest part of the training. Even now she wondered how far they could possibly have succeeded, those interrogators and white-coated analysts. Could she really talk to another person without prejudice, without anger, *sans* guilt?

They had all been very good natured about her doubts. Every question she had for them was scrupulously debated: first among themselves, then with her.

'All a matter of degree.' Nodding.

'Not an exact science.' Smiling.

Finally she decided that, after all, the message was rather simple: do the best you can. There was one aspect, however, they had explained very carefully to her several times. That it was not only her own personality that had been reprogrammed but also – how did they put it? – the evolved personality of the everywoman, the all, the collective.

She did feel differently. Different. She wondered how they could have done that without altering her memories.

She wondered, too, about the man. He was her partner in the experiment though they were yet to meet.

Even their senses had been skilfully refined. Now they could each hear a cat washing its face, smell a breeze that had passed over water. Only then were they allowed into the garden where they were left to wander around to do just what they felt they would do.

They were naked.

Each thought the garden perfect. The most majestic of trees were there – cedars, chestnut, giant oaks. They gave the place a sense of endurance: of age and wisdom. Both the weight and exuberance of summer spread before them. Wonderful contrasts of dappled light and shade. There were bright candles in the leaves where peep-holes of sun insisted they should be.

The landscape was soft. Rises and hollows laid down like the folds of a heavy cloak. A wide stream meandered through the trees, sometimes bursting into view as a path of crushed diamonds. A shallow stream, fast running and musical. Ancient polished stones made footpaths to the other side. Occasionally a stray curl of water painted their colours for a moment before the sun dried them again, quickly, as if dissatisfied and impatient to begin again before the inspiration was spent.

Neither of them affected surprise, nor indeed felt any, at seeing the other there. The woman was sitting quietly, arms about her knees, rocking gently. The man took up the same position opposite her. They looked calmly into each other's eyes.

'It's been a long time since we met,' he said.

'Yes, it has,' she agreed.

There followed a silence between them, the kind that comes of not being in a hurry.

Eventually the woman spoke. 'Do you think it is ever possible to start again?'

'I don't know.' The man smiled to himself, relishing such unaccustomed words. He continued...

'I think that is what nearly everyone is longing to do but first we must try to discover, if we can, what went wrong.'

The man invited the woman to speak first. She accepted the invitation simply on the grounds that an equitable discussion has to start somewhere.

'It all seemed so uncomplicated at the beginning. While you were preoccupied with the struggle for survival, we were just as busy providing sustenance and offspring. You were proud and sure. We marvelled at your ingenuity: the wheel, the Renaissance, washing machines.'

The man smiled, then bowed his head. 'Thank you. We felt proud of ourselves too. But that doesn't explain the rift between us. It seemed that the more convenient our lives were, the sorrier we became.'

The woman offered him a sad smile. 'Do you remember the cost of that progress? The mass slaughters of our sons and potential lovers? Miserable, sordid wars, in which the adversaries were more often rats than other men. We felt we must protest. Silence only condones atrocities.'

'Which, I recall, is exactly what you did. Then you promptly declared your own war ... against us.' He wondered for a moment if she would deny it.

'Yes ... that's right. We knew we ought to do something but it was hard to know what.'

'You mimicked us.'

'Did we?'

'Yes, don't you remember? You demanded sameness. You used your bras to symbolise liberation. "A call to arms," you shouted and we soon came to realise that you did not mean loving arms.'

She remained silent so he continued. 'Meanwhile, as our intellectual gladiators assembled in the arena to fling accusations and recriminations at each other a third force, bigger than you or I, decimated the rank and file of us. It was dreadful to see. It was all around us, a lurking, virile force – apathy, despair, helplessness, even suicide. All summed up in that catch phrase, "Oh God, what's it all about!"'

The woman adjusted her position, stretched out full length, leaning on one elbow. Having settled comfortably, she smiled at him. Encouraged, he went on...

'At the time when we were forging ahead so quickly in technology and science, we were comfortable with the false assumption that we were at the centre of a benign, infinitely perpetuating universe. As we raced up the escarpment towards what we thought was the summit, catastrophe struck us down with such an impact that we were thrown, writhing, to the ground. It was wrong of us to keep it from you, pointless, too, it showed up in our general behaviour. We had picked up knowledge like manna, masses of it, then suddenly our trusted beliefs evaporated – we were in touch with a more fatalistic divinity.'

The woman interrupted here. 'I don't think I understand what you mean.'

'Well, you see, we found this dreadful knowledge, we became aware that we might succumb to cosmic disaster, an asteroid collision, the sun becoming hotter before dying. The ending of all life on earth.'

'Oh, I see, black holes, light years and so on. Perhaps that accounts for the two extreme responses that we witnessed. On the one hand, building penile rockets with which you perhaps hoped to mate with the universe; and on the other, the growth of an anti-will that would eventually lead to total resignation – actually wanting the button to be pressed as a final solution to despair. Species suicide. First, though, we would have a party. Such a party. Hedonism and greed right up to the last choking breath.'

She touched his hand lightly. 'I didn't realise you were in such trouble.'

The man looked at his hand for several minutes. 'I think if you had done that before it would have helped.'

She sighed then. 'It is a natural gesture for me as a woman – it's as natural as your responses towards me. From the beginning of your days, my breast has been the perpetual symbol of succour and love. It is surely no accident of human behaviour that being pressed to the breast is the most potent source of comfort, both in times of distress and in times of overwhelming pleasure.'

The man looked at her breasts, feeling denied and sad. Mother breasts, woman breasts. Wanting both. Needing both.

She heard him speak again. 'It's true, what you say is true, but I feel you are mistaken in suggesting that such behaviour is the exclusive property of womanhood.'

This time she responded quickly: 'Indeed! Yet you seemed to feel that it was unmanly to weep, frivolous to gambol with delight.'

112

He laughed. She liked that. Then he was serious again. 'What I hear you saying now may be closer to the truth than we imagine. I suspect that we separated our roles so distinctly that for a time we deluded ourselves into thinking of each other as separate species?'

'Yes, go on, I hear something in that, too. I distinctly remember accusing you of not treating me as a person when what I really meant was that you were not treating me as a *woman*. I felt denigrated and left behind.'

'We can only personify being male or female. I think rather than that, we were so disgusted with each other that we no longer wanted to share the same identity. What we overlooked, though, was our failure to agree about the values we would attach to being either a female person or a male person.'

'There! You see? Becoming a person is important. It's being male or female that is incidental. I begin to feel proud of my sisters after all, though I did find some of their antics embarrassing. Let me try to describe to you how it was. I accept that you were in the throes of a malevolent despair. Women's voices become most strident when our progeny are threatened. Our shouts, muted by Valium, became whimpers. So we started to respond with various mental and physical symptoms of our growing panic. We raised experts but let ourselves become intimidated by them. With a passive exterior to a quickening alarm, we presumed they would see what was going on. So we waited. Finally, when the silence became claustrophobic, we reverted to primitive responses. A female creature, as you know, will leave her nest or lair if chronically disturbed. By now some of us fear to have children, some of us are harming our own offspring, many more of us are maligning all men hoping to make them carry the responsibility for our own shame...'

The man leaned forward. 'Forgive me for interrupting here, but I feel you are in danger of feeling contempt for yourself. I must share with you how it was for us – you may derive some comfort from the similarities. Our main palliatives were alcohol and aggression. When we came home to irascible wives, themselves contaminated by our hopelessness, we beat them, raped them, even on occasion mutilated them. Worst of all, like you, we turned against our own infants and calmly devoured them with bombs and grenades.'

The woman began to cry for them both. 'Please hold hands with me. Even in a place as beautiful as this the enormity of our evil makes me tremble.'

They held hands for many hours, stroking away the fear from faces and fingertips, wiping away the tears of repentance. Removed, as they had been, from the fearful consequences of guilt, they cried their way through to reconciliation. The woman finally composed herself and spoke again.

'We needn't have been so appalled by what Darwin proposed after all. It had a metaphysical implication that we overlooked – yet another signpost we ignored. No wonder you couldn't treat me as a woman ... I wasn't one. If you see me now only as mother or female, it is because I am the one who possesses the power and I am the one who failed to use it responsibly. I take the blame for this sorry mess, my dear.'

He did not contradict her but said, 'I will endeavour to be just as honest. We, too, misinterpreted Darwin, thought that "survival of the fittest" referred to physical prowess and attractiveness. We failed to acknowledge the one distinction between ourselves and all the other creatures: consciousness. Individual physique and superiority of munitions was our breeding call. We were like rutting stags. The rewards served to perpetuate these attitudes because in return for power, prestige, wealth, we got first choice of nubile girls. They, in turn, gilded their flanks for us, offered their breasts as trophies to confirm the delusion. When they conceived, we moved on to the next, leaving the first with resentments that were often visited on the child. We quite over-looked that we not only inherit physical characteristics but also attitudes: from generation unto generation. Survival of the fittest should have read 'survival of the fittest for the task'.

The woman shook her head ruefully. 'Are we now agreed on the task?'

'My suggestion is that we strive to become adults and take over our inheritance.'

'To become Gods in turn?'

'Yes.'

'That is where you and I come in. Neither of us can do it alone.'

'What you are suggesting, then, is that we become the vehicles as well as the possessors of what we seek?'

'Are we there yet?'

'Not quite...'

They were silent. Each recognised a rising excitement, not only because they seemed closer to what they were seeking, but also because in pursuing the same goal together they were working as equals. The sense of sameness warmed the air around them.

It was as if a paternal and maternal influence held an arm around each of their shoulders, hugging them together. It evoked a sense of reality and truth, which neither of them wanted to resist; a synthesis of ancient fragmented memories, a something that had persisted despite the distortions of history and of personal experience. The man spoke:

'I recall this emotion well. All descriptions of it are meagre compared to the experience, but if I try to describe even a nuance I think you will provide us both with the word that defines our task. There is a time in all our lives when we have the meaning of life within our grasp. We are generous. We seek the welfare of another individual beyond our own. We are quite certain of being understood and valued. For however long this delightful, bewitching state lasts we feel totally worthy of the unqualified regard in which we are held. Our very senses are purified. Colours and sounds intoxicate us. Sometimes we can barely tolerate the joy and suffer it as an exquisite pain. We cannot be still, life is full of plan and purpose. We worship the object of these emotions.'

She did not hesitate. 'Love.'

'Love.'

He thought that in all his life he had never seen a more beautiful smile than the one she gave him then, nor heard such music in a voice.

'Let me endorse what you say. We, too, can never forget what ecstasy is like. From then on, we project the memory onto landscapes and places. We see it reflected in sea and lake because we recall its safety and comfort as in the waters of my pregnant womb and the primeval waters of creation. All the doubts we have discussed between us here become redundant – everything has meaning. It takes many forms but we cannot lose hope when it evolves between a man and a woman.'

'Perhaps that is why it is only a glimpse,' he said sadly. 'I think we have a little further to go with this. As usual, we fall into the trap of regarding ourselves as central to the issue. But this secret, like all others, is not exclusive to us. It is revived in every birdsong. Each spring pays tribute to it. When it fails, as it does when we devalue it, we pursue it, again and again, with the restlessness of loss and, for some of us, the anger and resentment of bereavement.'

'You suggest, then, that love is not enough?'

'Not at all! Only that I feel we need to consolidate these glimpses into a way of life for us as individuals and for us as the species, however long it takes.'

'Then we must view it as the goal as well as the task. I shall start tomorrow. In future, I shall look to the man who is intent on becoming wise. I will measure his stature by his love of himself, rather than in centimetres. I will look for his acts of love without reference to gender and provide him with sons and daughters in that image. I shall take full responsibility for his successes and his failures. Each time he becomes complacent or falsely believes that his own mischievous thoughts and actions belong to someone else, he will admit it as a revelation. And each time he does so I shall applaud him.'

They hugged each other. He whispered in her ear: 'How will you recognise him?'

'I shall feel the warmth.'

At this point the conductor raised her baton ... and waited. She is prepared to wait for ever...

Chapter 15

After I had written down those ideas I felt much calmer. I also felt guilty: after all, it wasn't as if I hadn't seen and heard it all before...

'But I thought you were happy.'

'You should have seen the signs.'

'You should have told me what was wrong.'

'You should have noticed.'

I had sensed the trap, was frightened again. Oh, Pat, you are so easily frightened still.

I thought of Russian women, encouraged to restore the population after the devastating losses in the war. Twenty children – dying early – heroines of the State. Other women, timid, selfless. Overburdened donkey women, resting at last, nice tombstone; healthy, selfish offspring, gathered around the chiselled inscription: 'She was a good woman'. Not meaning it.

Very good. Very fine. Now tell me the point of knowing what you 'don't' want if you cannot say what it is you 'do' want!

'No need to be sarcastic about it.'

'Well?!'

'All right!'

'Supposing he turns out to be the man of my fears? Supposing I turn out to be the woman of his fears?'

'Get to the point, girl!'

'I'm scared. OK? Happy now? I'm scared.'

'Go talk to the boulder.'

'What!?

Look in a mirror. Choose what you think is a flattering photograph; still, you might not recognise yourself if you were to meet along a path. No matter how you think you present to the world, it is rarely the truth of who you really are. For the truth of that, we can only rely on how the world relates to us. Usually it is a reasonable assessment, like it or not. But it is *you* who is responsible for presenting the evidence.

Enter the real world, Pat. It is time to leave the past behind. Stop hiding. Don't try so hard. After all, neither of us would make worthy delegates, but it didn't mean that we couldn't grow with the boat...

There were a couple of matters to deal with first before I could get going again.

First, I kicked the boulder hard. It hurt my foot – no more than I deserved. Then I turned my back on it and never referred to it again.

Second, I had my own private talk with the boat. Made it mean as much to me as it did to Ken.

'Keep us together, please. Keep us together until we are both mended.'

Things changed then. In sharing a total commitment to the building of the boat, our attitudes altered. As with most forms of liberating change, it was sometimes uncomfortable both physically and emotionally but it did prove to us that men and women can see goals through together and that the best bit is the together bit.

We never overlooked the fact that we were a man and a woman, nor did we succeed in eliminating all the silly games played out between the sexes but those that remain have the more healthy air of banter about them. We were able to reduce some of the conflicts we all endure. In particular those between apathy and enterprise, men and women, 'I wish' dreams and 'I will' dreams.

It was in those early days that I stumbled and doubted ... the historical prejudice about a female presence in a boat-yard. Precision instruments will be treated like tin openers, dangerous tools as if they are bowls of flowers. The sneaky practice of sidling past me – too often for reasonable excuse or passion – just to see what I was up to. In those days, if I shattered a light bulb or a drill bit? Carelessness. When he did the same? Bad luck.

But there would come the later days ... working together without intrigue or politics. No one to tell us off for watching the goldfinches feeding off the thistles when we should have been working. An unspoken acknowledgement that our skills and temperament could be different yet still be complementary.

All that I believed in. Everything I had ever wanted...

Chapter 16

'Feeling better, love?' Ken had noticed that my boots were standing next to his again.

'Yes, thanks, I've been overdoing it a bit.' I held up one of his boots to make the point. 'We won't need a tender, will we? Let's just put an outboard onto one of these.'

I picked up one of my boots and placed it right inside one of his until it disappeared into the toe. 'I'm not as big as you, Ken, not as strong as you.'

Ken took the boots from me and set them down again. 'Come back inside, let's have another cup of coffee before we go.'

Ken made the coffee. Unusual. 'I knew you were getting tired,' he said, 'but I thought if I said anything you might get annoyed.'

'You noticed though!'

'Of course.'

'That's all that matters.' I smiled, feeling ridiculously pleased.

'Don't overdo it, Pat. I don't want you doing that. It's just that I forget how big I am.'

I took him at his word. Yet something about casting off resentments had given me extra energy so that I found myself working harder than ever. Able to – wanting to.

If resentment soaks up energy so does lack of money. Not being able to afford a loaf of bread is about as energy sapping as it gets. Our somewhat fatalistic approach towards money would certainly not suit everyone: nor do we have the temerity to suggest that it should. I suppose we flew in the face of most conventions where money was concerned and for that kind of indiscretion there is a price to pay. The question was not so much whether the boat could survive, but could we? Yet we have only to think back to the oak tree, the axle and the engine to feel that maybe the innocent have charmed lives.

If our situation was difficult, sometimes even dire, it was never complicated. We simplified our lifestyle to the point where we discovered that what we once thought of as needs were almost invariably wants.

For weeks at a time we learned to manage quite happily on cream crackers instead of bread, potatoes and cheese instead of meat. Our friends were more than willing to provide us with second-hand clothes. We were always so enthusiastic about them despite the exaggerated squabble about who would claim the sweaters. Sweaters were negotiable. Trousers, for obvious reasons, were not.

Fortunately holidays held no fascination for either of us. If we felt a need for rest and recuperation we did something slightly less arduous, but then again we have always been prepared to down tools for an amiable chat, and most of our days were pleasantly interrupted in that way.

To compensate for these frugal ways, we occasionally indulged ourselves – a Fry's Cream bar for a treat, a tin of sliced peaches made to last two days for a double treat. Transport to the yard was an unavoidable expense but we rarely paid more than ten or twenty pounds for a vehicle and Ken could keep any car roadworthy, even when the mileage had registered its first 100,000 miles, which it generally had.

Using our boiler suits as badges of competence, we volunteered for any type of work providing we could do it together: roofing, paving, decorating, welding, making equipment and tanks for other boats. There is something unpredictable, even adventurous, about intermittent work, but fortunes vary considerably and there are penalties to be paid for taking liberties in a social climate that is organised around greed. You generally work harder for fewer wages; also you will only be paid for what is seen to be done. The 'executive' costs such as travelling to the job or running around for materials could not be charged for by the likes of us. I recall one old lady who led us a very merry dance.

We agreed to mend her front step, which was wobbling and therefore dangerous for her. It would only take a couple of hours. The materials were cheap enough so we gave her an estimate of £5. By the time we had joined the queue at the local builders' trade counter, then the queue of cars waiting to join the motorway, mixed the cement and settled the wobbling step, half a day was gone. Not that it mattered – we needed the £5 urgently to buy some brass screws. A feeling for social work led us to make a wooden ramp so as not to inconvenience the old dear while the cement set.

Finally we knocked on the door for our pay.

'I wonder ... while you are here ... one of those paving slabs is moving, too ... and could you get the leaves off the bit of grass at the back...'

Having neglected to identify which slab she was talking about, we checked them all. Perhaps she realised that we would feel honour bound to reset every one that moved. There were nine of them. Repairing to the back garden, we duly raked up all the leaves, much to the aggravation and annoyance of more toads to the square yard than there are mole hills to the acre. We popped them under her privet hedge, covering each one with a charity blanket of the damp leaves.

At last we were paid our £5. Counted out slowly into Ken's hand. Looking on, I couldn't judge which of the hands was shaking the most: the arthritic one ... or the embarrassed one. Each carefully folded note would be sorely missed from the weekly budget. We squirmed with guilt. Why couldn't the old lady just have handed us a box of screws. We made sure that she did not know how to get in touch with us again. We might take pride in a reputation that our work was conscientious, definitely good value for money, but in this case we preferred that she did not recommend us to her friends!

As we drove home I reflected on how ungracious society had become. My mother had always taken tea and cake to anyone working odd jobs for her. She had a favourite story about it. She made delectable caraway seed cake once a week for dad. There was a man rotavating the vegetable patch on the day she baked so she cut a couple of slices into the cake so that he could take a piece for himself. 'I was showing off.' She giggled so much telling this story that I would ask her to tell it over and over just to hear it. 'It was just the right colour, beautiful cake, I wanted him to admire the whole thing.'

She would become helpless then, gales and peals of laughter. 'Do you know what he did? He left the two slices and took the whole of the rest of the cake. He did! Honestly, he did!'

'Didn't you say anything to him, Mum?' I always said that on cue so that she could deliver the last line.

'Not a word, I was so flabbergasted I couldn't say a word. When he brought the plate back he said how much he had enjoyed it!'

And here we had been working for a whole day and not even the offer of a cup of water. Oh well.

In ways like this we survived for the first few years of the project, keeping our personal needs to a bare minimum, learning to treat time like a fellow conspirator. It might take Ken several weeks to design then fabricate a single item for the boat. But it was time that had to be set aside against the months it would otherwise take to earn the hundreds of pounds to pay for the manufactured version. Besides which, our trust in what was handmade was absolute.

The latter stages of any yacht's construction, self built or otherwise, are unavoidably expensive. There are many aspects to a boat that are beyond the scope of do-it-yourself: paint, plywood, glue, navigation equipment. Whenever we dared look that far, one fact seemed inevitable: we would have to take a couple of years out to earn a more substantial income. Our timetable would run into more than a decade. Perhaps too long…

That reality was upon us sooner than we expected. Everything needing to be prepared for the interior shot-blasting was ready. Ken had gone as far as he could by making his own shot-blasting equipment. Starting with a bare air cylinder he added an ingenious arrangement of gas barrel circuitry and gate valves. Even so, the kitty would not support the cost of hiring a road compressor, nor even one bag of grit.

What we would never do was borrow money or go on the dole. Having volunteered for a way of life, the hardships we encountered were of our own making – we must accept all the consequences. If we leaned in and out of the system just to suit ourselves the boat would, after all, fail to reflect the spirit that moved us so purposefully. Win or lose, it must depend entirely on our own efforts; borrowing money would be a serious blemish. In return we hoped to be tolerated as being slightly barmy but no harm to anyone.

We sat up late in the caravan discussing our predicament. How could we get substantial work where Ken did not have to complete a form in triplicate or where I didn't need to wear a skirt? By now neither of us possessed a single garment that could be termed respectable. Was there something we could make and sell? Above all, was there something we could do in an enlightened industrial climate so that we might continue to work together. In the hidden agenda was the question of whether this was the time to consider the word 'Impossible'.

We were getting some pretty negative answers to all of these questions before the knock on the door and the bit of hearsay from a friend. There might be a couple of weeks work for a pair of welders, he told us, if we turned up at an industrial estate early next morning. We hardly slept.

The huge undertaking that was about to come our way not only solved most of our immediate financial problems but also put the crowning smile on the face of providence. But we earned every single penny.

Chapter 17

I suppose it was a bit childish to have introduced ourselves to the business partner as the 'A' team. We thought it might be the right sort of pleasantry to break the ice since the man appeared to be struggling: some kind of conflict was going on, between horror and good manners. We thought wrong. Trying to disguise our anxiety by appearing confident only seemed to make matters worse. This was evident from the brittle silence that followed our remark.

His head leaned so far back from his neck we feared it might topple. We tried to see it from his point of view: what an unlikely looking pair! What Tom and Jerry, Owl and the Pussy Cat sort of cartoon was *this*?!

All credit to him for overcoming his surprise; then again, he may have wondered whether there was entertainment value in giving it a try. Anyway, he suggested that we ring the 'governor' (i.e. he who pays the wages) that evening to offer him our terms. He wanted a grain mill built and we would be part of a large labour force for the job.

We agonised over what we should charge for our labour. Too much and the opportunity would be lost. Too little would compromise our credibility. It was altogether unreasonable to think that the partner could tell, just by looking at us, that we could handle the job. Indeed he was probably doubting his sense already; what he thought he had seen was surely just a sign of tiredness or stress?

It was finally agreed that we would charge the same fixed hourly rate for both of us, whatever the day of the week, whatever the number of hours a day. Ken flatly refuses to work 'for' anyone; he will only work 'with' you.

After he had spoken to Peter Turner on the telephone that

evening he was a happy man. Not only were the terms accepted as eminently fair, but he also learned that Peter was a man who had built up a small business entirely through his own hard work and was now prepared to risk all by buying a new industrial unit to expand his horizons. Time was of the essence to him: every day spent on the new project was essential income lost.

An irresistible situation. Nothing could be fairer – his dream for ours.

Neither of us is prepared to feign modesty about the building of that mill. It was a prodigious feat in every way. In five months, working ten hours a day, seven days a week, we erected a Crystal Palace structure in steel, 25 tons of it. More than enough to build another boat.

There were no plans for the mill, just a few line drawings on a postcard. A perfect situation for Ken. He was bouncing and straining like a dog on a lead, the ball just inches from his twitching nose. He thought through the whole milling process so that he could design it as a one-man operation. Each of the nine 15-ton capacity hoppers was suspended inside a massive support structure, lined out in thin gauge steel, then pop-riveted. Six thousand holes to drill.

The promised labour force never materialised; in the end it was just as well. Ken held the idea in his head; it would have been counterproductive to 'boss' the job and have to explain every step in the construction to others. I didn't need bossing. Ken added a bit – I welded it – ten hours a day.

We became rather precious about the whole thing, almost as if it were another boat. Success with the mill symbolised success with our own project and we badly needed to imagine what it might be like to pack up the tools one day, look back and finally see what we had made. The mill was a supremely satisfying rehearsal of a day still long in the future when we would raise the mainsail of *Imago*.

For the first couple of weeks we were something of a novelty on the rest of the industrial estate. I suspect it was as much because of our impudence in taking on the job as the fact that we were a husband and wife team. Men would take their tea breaks in the doorway, watching in silence as we scrambled about the structure like a pair of monkeys or leaned perilously from the fork-lift hoist close to the ceiling 22 feet up in the air. A height at which I was sure I needed oxygen!

Ken believes that I was the main attraction. I felt it was more a curiosity about the working relationship we enjoyed than about the work I was seen to do. Whatever opinions were around, I was never subjected to barracking or leers. I wish I could have let them know how grateful I was about that.

There is no doubt that Ken was my protection against ribald comment but I still like to think that we blew a gentle wind of change in some directions. I never felt threatened or embarrassed. Even Ken, who hasn't a prejudiced notion in his head, was surprised that he was never called upon to defend me. He put it down to the fact that being quiet by nature and small there was nothing in my demeanour that could possibly be construed as a challenge.

There were occasional problems. Driving the fork-lift came second nature to Ken: just another vehicle to drive. My management of it remained unpredictable to the end. At least seven levers to operate inside the cab was just too many by five.

One day I caught his foot in the hoist arm then proceeded to squash it a little flatter each time I chose a lever. It was at least four levers later before I eventually released his foot from medieval torture. There followed quite a heated exchange of views, what with him bellowing in fear and me insisting I was 'trying'.

'Your foot shouldn't have been there in the first place!' I pointed out.

'You panicked!'

'You were shouting at me!'

Classic matrimonial trench warfare, but we could always laugh at each other when the danger had passed. The possibility of serious injury had not occurred to us before so it was agreed that the incident should serve as a useful reminder.

The construction environment is still an unusual experience for most women. While I was saddened, even offended, by the colossal waste of materials, it was a privilege to witness what is left of craftsmanship and to overhear splendid examples of witty banter.

Men gathered together are irrepressibly rude to each other though offence is rarely taken provided the taboo subjects are avoided: stuff like shared girlfriends, physical characteristics or the morals of your mother; otherwise plenty of latitude. Most exchanges are brutally honest. Outright criticism is never dressed up in polite language or subtle innuendo. A meaty 'airing of views' would rattle around and ricochet like gunfire – quick, semi-automatic fire. Conversely, it was quite normal to see a group of men in a huddle, totally at ease, yet saying nothing. Different to women, I thought. We tend to prefer polite over honest. And as for a group of silent women? Pass.

I discovered that a boiler suit is a passport: honourable garb in the environment of factories, grease nipples, explicit calendars, male and female couplings of the engineering sort. As we journeyed round the estate during our lunch breaks, Ken was at home, tall and easy among his peers, while I discovered that the other side are not as hostile as the propaganda suggests. Best of all were the rare and privileged excursions to workshop dens inhabited by craftsmen and their cobwebs. It was like sighting a rare species on the edge of extinction. Such craftsmanship is a pleasure to witness and serves to check the arrogance of young men, even today when swaggering appears to be the media choice of adolescent attitudes. You do not earn the title chippie, spreader, brickie, spiderman or sparks other than from your peers in the game, and to earn the respect implied by those terms you must be very good indeed.

Calendar girls were everywhere. Contrary to what the advertisers would have us believe there are no archetypes. The girls portrayed are fat, thin, nubile, mature, blonde, brunette, innocent, knowing. Someone for everyone and the longing universal. Sex objects we are. Denial is fruitless. Real power, girls!

I don't know what came over me! The Motor Show was on at the time. There were the usual magazine spreads portraying shiny symbols of potency with gilded female 'trophies' draped all over the bonnets. Made you wonder what was meant by supercharged, though the Formula One winners and their effervescing champagne bottles isn't all that subtle either!

I was telling Ken about some particularly explicit magazine I had found stuffed behind the plumbing pipes in the toilet. It was late in the evening. The estate was eerily silent. Just the occasional sharp bark of a patrolling guard dog. We were alone in the building with all the doors shuttered fast.

The first support structure was illuminated by the halogen lamp, throwing stark shadows against the retaining wall. Ken, who always carries his camera, decided it would make a moody photograph. We chatted away while he took the pictures and as I went round switching off the apparatus, before leaving for the day.

'I wonder why nude girls are never included in advertisements for tractors or fork-lifts,' I remarked.

'Why not piston rings or fishing reels?' added Ken.

Suddenly I had a clear image in my mind of a ridiculous Motor Show spoof. Without much further ado, my clothes lay in a pile at my feet. I climbed up on the fork-lift and posed! Well, there is an art to it after all – my posing did nothing to enhance either me or the fork-lift. I couldn't get the hang of the limp draping so favoured by the glossies. My posture was stiff and self-conscious. Nor did I feel in the least bit sexually provocative, which is not too surprising when you consider that I was leaning against cold steel on a November evening: not to mention all those levers!

But, the advertisers are right after all. There was my own dear husband, arty shot of shadows on a wall instantly rejected in favour of his silly nude wife posing daftly and stiff as a brick across the cab of a fork-lift!

The resulting pictures left a lot to be desired. Hollywood would not be ringing me. It was only when I heard the excuses that I came to fully realise how powerful are the works of market research. Ken's hands were sweating and he had camera shake! I should say here that I am not deformed in any way but neither am I a Kate Moss nor a Victoria Beckham, or ever expected a call from Hollywood!

It is quite beyond me to fathom it out, but I do confess that it felt wonderfully wicked and daring, while also free and totally innocent. A delicious spur of the moment piece of nonsense.

The wages for our work were squirreled away to await our return to the boat, when we would be free for more than a year to buy essential materials just as they were needed.

On the last day at the mill, we decorated the structure with bunting and I set our names and the date into the steel with weld.

'Ken / Pat 1984.'

Every time we returned to do odd jobs in the rest of the building, we stared at what we had done with disbelief. Today we still look at the boat in much the same way.

The unaccustomed wealth served as a much needed boost to our confidence despite the fatigue of working so long without a break. A shopping list of priorities was drawn up: paint, plywood, a sextant, echo sounder and log, screws by the boxload, and enough in reserve for fabric. We would buy a sail-maker's sewing machine when a second-hand one came our way. Eight pounds a week to keep the intrepid pair alive for a year – now we would make spectacular progress.

In just a few more weeks the fitting out would start. To celebrate such a milestone we bought ourselves brand new boilers in pristine white: 'chippies' garb. We were carpenters now. We thought ourselves so smart that we went to dinner in them, to some dear indulgent friends living in the most salubrious part of Sunningdale in Berkshire. I felt particularly elegant since these were the first boilers that had not been hand-me-downs; the first I actually wore rather than wrapped around me. Proud as an astronaut, I was!

But after the private viewing they were carefully packed away. There was still the job to do that we shall always remember as the one that stretched our personalities to the limit. At least we could say at the end that it was a triumph for our marriage...

Chapter 18

The shot-blaster itself was a very special example of the 'make what you cannot afford to buy' principle. Both in looks and in personality it resembled a Dalek. As with all hand-crafted apparatus it possessed idiosyncrasies all of its own. In Ken's hands it showed dog-like faithfulness; towards anyone else it was just as consistently obnoxious. Just as well really ... I didn't particularly want to be friends with it though I admired it enormously.

We all wondered whether Ken had gone too far this time. Even Richard offered a dire warning that our lives would soon be over, and a messy business altogether, what with our corpuscles and molecular structure spread over a large area of the boat's interior. Mick, too, made himself scarce. 'I want to grow up to be a jockey,' he said to me.

'What do you mean?'

'I want to grow up ... you know ... live a bit longer.'

I hugged him, 'Have faith, Mick.' But the words did not come out as lightly as they should have done.

It was a precision instrument of course (Daleks are rather vain). The correct balance between pressure and volume was critical, as was the need to learn the dual skills of paint sprayer and fireman. Wounds caused by grit under pressure are both dangerous and painful. Unless the hose was kept firmly under control, it would assume a playful disposition and try to blast the clothes off your back. Hence the need for a fireman's skills because if it did escape it could only be restrained by a rugby tackle three inches from its spiteful little throat!

I wondered what could possibly be more masochistic than having to wear sweaters, long johns, oilskins, wellington boots and welding gauntlets, with the summer all golden outside, the temperature in the eighties. Did I mention, too, the adapted motor cycle helmet?

Ken was my hero, so naturally I treated him as one. Each time he emerged from the cloud of rust particles and three-inch visibility I mopped him with a towel, wrung it out, mopped him again. With heartless indifference (heroes don't like a fuss made, you see) I replaced the lens in his helmet, then pushed him back into the torment. My own support work was quite enough for me to handle. There was no room in either of our hearts for compassion.

At the end of each blasting session of 20 minutes or so, I went aboard with the Hoover and hand brush to collect the iron filings that were spread, ankle deep, over the whole cabin area. Once collected, as if that were not enough, they had then to be passed laboriously through a sieve so that they could be used several more times.

While Ken rested and sweated between rounds, I cleaned up and prepared for the next session by cutting fresh lenses from a thin sheet of perspex (the ricochets would make them opaque again within minutes). While I rested and sweated, he went back to the front line.

The blaster worked like a dream. Thirty to forty square feet could be cleaned in one forty-minute session. Having such a portable apparatus enabled us to work in optimum conditions when air humidity was low. Excluding all moisture makes for an almost perfect procedure when applying paint to steel. We also avoided wasted hire charges since the compressor could be brought in at short notice when weather conditions were optimal.

I was given sole managerial responsibility for this beast since 'on' and 'off' were clearly labelled, as was the lever that regulated the air flow. Matters had improved somewhat since the day of the squashed foot. Still, just in case, we employed a set of signals – two taps on the hull and I was to start up the compressor; two screams and I was to turn it off.

Between us we went to the local cottage hospital five times in the six weeks it took to complete the job. Steel grit is excruciatingly painful if you get it in your eye. Even after the eyeball has been gruesomely scraped, then washed clean, it still hurts for days. A careless sweep with the hand brush, or wiping the nose on the edge of a rusty shirtsleeve was all it took. The route to the hospital became so familiar we could have travelled blindfold, which, as it turned out, was just as well.

Inadvertent, it was. He leaned into the polythene sheeting that hung as a barrier to keep the grit out of the forward cabin. A good kilo of the stuff cascaded from a fold in the material filling both his eyes right to the brim! I kept absolute silence as he held both hands out so that I could lead him to the car and thence to the hospital, only giving vent to my mirth during the drive back with my companion and his two sailor's eye patches.

'Oh, it's you again, Mrs Gogay,' the casualty sister had accused.

'No, it's the other one this time, Sister,' I said truculently, pointing to the one who looked like a deep-sea diver. I guided him through the swing doors into her presence.

'You both seem to be rather careless in your work,' she observed.

'There you are!' I whispered to Ken as he lay groaning on the couch, 'You heard what Sister said ... careless!'

He grinned and tried to grab at where he heard the cheek coming from but by then I had skipped to Sister's side where I spoke in the most solicitous terms. 'I think he's delirious, sister ... a shot of morphine, perhaps?'

I didn't hear the word 'careless' for a long time after that.

Blind or not, the boat must now be painted quickly to take full advantage of such a sound preparation. We used an epoxy coal tar system inside. Ex-Admiralty stock so we reckoned on the highest specification. It retailed at £33 for five litres but we found some at a surplus store for £10, which allowed us to apply two thick coats for about £100. While there is no doubt that meticulous preparation is worthwhile, the do-it-yourself version is a murky, dirty, labour-intensive job. By the end of it we were as bone tired as we had ever been.

*   *   *

At long last we had a hull and superstructure to fit out. The very point at which most amateur boat-builders begin. We have both long forgotten whether that seemed a daunting prospect or not.

As well as welder and fabricator of steel, Ken must now become interior designer, electrician, carpenter, plumber, upholsterer, mechanic, rigger and toolmaker. By now, I knew him well enough to realise that it was as much the challenge that inspired him as the ever-present economic constraints. His faithfulness to the do-it-yourself principle and the integrity with which he can claim that he built his boat himself was total. Even if he had come into riches he would not have changed his approach.

In a little under two weeks the tent under the bow was converted into a carpenter's shop lined out with an impressive array of handmade machine tools. Instead of steel grit and lubricating oil in the sandwiches we now had to adapt to the flavour of sawdust and the odd brass screw – size eight usually!

For each piece of machinery, he bought only the essential components. The first of these was a set of planing blades and a tungsten-tipped circular saw. For safety, they were built into a steel box housing before being suspended inside a metal framework. With a system of pulleys and flanges each could be belt driven by the two angle grinders that had become redundant. That pleased me: I liked the thought of those monsters strapped and tied.

The same with the very useful face sander comprising a spinning disc 14 inches in diameter faced with fairly coarse production paper. This was powered by a one-horse electric motor, another of the precious trophies from the scrapyard. When Ken had lifted it up in triumph I told him to put it back! Rust was falling from it like dandruff. He insisted. I should have known better. After a day in the shed it emerged looking exactly the same but proceeded to serve us without fail during four years of almost daily use. For curves, angles and shaving off minute amounts of wood from a joint edge it was an invaluable tool.

None of these handmade tools ever let us down. It was the

production-made jigsaws and drills that burned out within a few short months.

Later on we acquired a rather grand piece of equipment to add to the collection. It boasted a gruesome history as a laboratory band-saw used in the pathology department for cutting sections of craniums and limbs. No amount of rubbing and scrubbing could rid it of certain rust-coloured stains. An imposing brass plate identified it as a genuine surgical instrument. It inevitably became the focus of dark humour, and we promptly called it the 'consultant' and treated it with due respect.

The tools set up, white boilers donned, we were ready to begin fitting out our hull.

The plans included general suggestions about the fitting out but omitted to supply essential information about detail and scale, so we dispensed with them altogether and designed the interior to suit our particular purpose.

Back to the three main objectives: a comfortable permanent home, a long-distance ocean-going craft, and a workshop that would maintain our vessel and help finance our travels. My contribution to the debate was to request a sizeable galley, large enough to accommodate a domestic cooker yet compact enough to be incorporated into the main saloon – no isolated cooks in crammed passageways on this craft!

To give us extra living space we decided to reduce the berths to five (one double, three singles); the last thing we wanted was submarine quarters below when for all our time at sea there would only be two of us aboard.

To get the feel of the woodwork and the different tools we would be using, it was decided that we should make doors first, though in truth we were both itching to see how the oak tree had weathered.

So many of the 2,500 days that passed while building the boat have now merged together as summers do in childhood, but the key memories still resurrect the emotions from that time as clearly as the episodes themselves. The fall of the oak tree always held a special significance. Now, at last, its time had come...

After four years of seasoning, the planks looked as nondescript as old scaffold boards. With suppressed excitement, we picked one from the pile that was the right thickness for the door frames, feeding it first through the band-saw to give us a length, then across the planer.

Two runs through removed the weathering to reveal the 'mighty oak' of poets. It was the transformation we had hoped for, and so very much more. In its raw state, English oak (white oak as the old shipwrights called it) is very pale. The grain is flecked and stippled as if from absentminded brush strokes. On what we called our 'specimen pieces' the quarter sawing revealed pearly smudges that caught the light like shot silk. With the first coat of sanding sealer the oak turned gold, the grain appeared like water patterns on parchment paper: light brown, pale apricot, opalescent, according to the light.

Monet? Turner? Constable? Wonderful works, movingly beautiful, but so was this – I never once tired of applying that first coat.

Chapter 19

Our first woodwork was of the highest standard. As amateur carpenters we were delighted with the results. The saloon doors had panelling in half-inch solid oak, tongue and grooved together, seams hardly visible. For the hanging locker doors we spent a whole day making handmade slats to provide a louvred panel both for ventilation and good looks.

Magnificent pieces, each of them, yet if we had maintained such a meticulous standard it would not only have taken at least ten years to fit out the boat but also we would have very quickly run out of tree!

Exactly the same thing was happening on all the other boats. There was the same sheepish talk about 'compromise here and there'. None of us wanted production boat interiors but nor did we have boats large enough to justify millionaire layouts. As time went by, even Des, the craftsman, was prepared to admit that a few of his joints were at least a 'thou' wider than hairline.

Fortunately this magnifying glass and micrometer phase lasted only a few weeks until it was realised that an inch-deep tenon joint gave more than adequate strength, that a door framed in oak but panelled in teak-faced plywood was every bit as attractive and a quarter the work.

Before any of the woodwork could be fixed and glued in place we had to decide about insulation. Urea-formaldehyde foam, sprayed on, was the technique recommended but the process cost several pounds per square metre. We could not afford it. We decided on the next best material – polystyrene. Even so, the number of two-inch thick sheets we would need added up to £250. In our scheme of things a sum like that represented a small fortune: we could live for more than 30 weeks on that. After the usual period spent fretting and worrying, concluding for the hundredth time that the whole idea was impossible, the solution came to mind.

Industrial skips don't just stand outside engineering firms, they also collect waste from office blocks and large retail firms. Over the next two days we collected washing machine and portable computer packaging by the van load. We simply introduced ourselves and said that we were building a boat. Just that – no details. Two of the directors we met even left their desks to show us the way. The only way to properly acknowledge such gestures was to succeed in launching and sailing the boat.

I remember feeling somewhat disgruntled about yet another long job of preparation before we could get on with the 'real' fitting out, but a chore like that needed my temperament. So I was renamed Polly Styrene and have forgotten how many ... many weeks it took.

We were expert by now in allocation of labour and had learned how best to encourage each other. While I packed in the insulation I could see Ken out of the corner of my eye preparing the beams for the head linings. The prospect of seeing those in place was exactly the right incentive to keep me going.

Every square inch from deck head to waterline is a huge area. By the time it was only half completed, we stood several inches deep in drifts of styrene particles. Lighter than dust, it floated up at the slightest disturbance, like the snow scene in a paperweight. Electrically charged particles, a universe of them. Although they stuck fast to every surface, they were especially attracted to skin. However much you brushed it away from mouth and eyes it simply bounced in the air like dandelion seed before settling back again in much the same spot. A mere trace of muttering led to a prolonged bout of energetic spitting, followed by a blizzard. So on the whole it was silent work to the strains of squeaking polystyrene inside and the high-pitched whine of saw and router outside – about as lovely as a heat-warped violin played with a comb.

We wanted that rarity – a warm, dry boat. As a further precaution we pasted cooking foil onto the back of every panel of plywood that was set against the hull and superstructure. This would serve to reflect excessive heat from outside as well as creating another barrier against warm air reaching the cold steel.

Wood is a warm and beautiful material to work with but steel is far more good natured. An error in steel is soon rectified by welding on a bit more then grinding it smooth. Not so with wood. All boat-builders are privy to a universal truth: all lengths trimmed to suit are exactly right or they are too short … never … ever … too long! It was just as well that we had a whole tree to play with, though the percentage error would decrease dramatically over time. The large bin euphemistically labelled 'offcuts' turned out to be a useful storage facility where 'failed' door stiles became fiddles, where 'failed' fiddles became catch blocks for the cupboard doors!

As beautiful and prophetic as the oak tree was, it exacted a price, as if to serve as a constant reminder of its origins. This most durable of woods is both dense and hard. Converting it from raw state to finished piece was a very time-consuming process, as was the constant resharpening of blunted planing blades and chisels. I suppose we should have invested in a belt sander but I genuinely preferred to sit crosslegged and prepare each piece by hand, starting with coarse paper, through the grades to fine.

Despite such a laborious approach, with many items taking days, even weeks to prepare, it did nothing to impede our progress. Ken's work was no less painstaking and we always kept pace with each other. His responsibilities were infinitely more demanding than mine. I do not say that to devalue my work in any way – we both knew its worth. It is simply true. My contribution as preparer and finisher was just that. The burden of design, proportion, which way a door should swing, all rested with Ken and his innate know-how. As with the steel work, we both slipped easily into a routine that made the most of what we each did best.

Ken accepts without demur that his painting and preparation

of wood is, to say the best, undistinguished. I can accept with the same equanimity that, even today, I remain largely ignorant of method. Even if I had made a door or a cabinet it would take a disproportionate amount of time and not be pleasing to the eye. The system that evolved therefore was the one that worked: Ken designed, framed up, skinned out in teak, then bounced into something new, leaving me to make trim and fiddles, plug holes, seal and finally set in the hinges and catches.

No two boat interiors are the same, just as no two living-rooms or kitchens are alike, but the basic contents are common to each. As the house will have a bathroom and bedrooms, so will a boat have heads and cabins. Strange then that the really hard part to fitting out would be deciding where everything should go.

It was a problem common to all the builders in the yard. Just like Ken, they would often spend a whole morning or afternoon sitting in gnawing anxiety, staring at a void in their boats that must transform itself into a galley or a shower area. We all knew that the galley should lie amidships where movement in rough seas is marginally less; that the best berths are in the stern, the least comfortable in the bow, but what about lockers, storage space, access for maintenance, headroom, hand holds? Where, how deep, how high, how big? Endlessly. Whatever the eventual proportions, they must fit the size of the vessel. The superbly spacious layout in that 60-footer you saw at the London Boat Show simply cannot be accommodated in a 40-foot sailboat.

Without question these were some of the hardest and most testing times for Ken. He could never focus his mind on one thing at a time. It was he who had to anticipate every facet of how his boat would function. It must be powered, fuelled, steered. It must be lighted, ventilated, made navigable. All those aspects of a boat's performance that do, and should, take preference over comfort and appearance.

Not surprising, then, that he would later suffer the debilitating symptoms of mental and physical saturation, that the last heartbreaking yards of his marathon would prove to be the longest of them all.

Perhaps now is the right moment to comment on some of the boat-building accounts that we came across in books and magazines. Some suggested that any reasonably competent individual can fit out a moderately sized vessel in six months! That particular article was passed around the boat-yard but failed to convince anyone that we were all miserable failures. It is simply not true. Nor was it helpful – there were enough casualties each season to say so. To suggest that fitting out a hull is just another spare time diversion causes many a soul to walk sadly or angrily away from their dream.

Being a small yard, we cannot fairly claim to be representative in the statistical sense; perhaps, too, some of the accounts may have presumed a labour force. We can only say that the boats around us were fitted out by a pattern maker, a carpenter, an electronics engineer, even a pair of shipwrights and that the average time taken was a little under three years. In each case, it involved working consistently for most evenings and every weekend.

For the most part, Ken and I – between earning sufficient funds to provide for daily needs and materials – laboured seven days a week. The boat-yard was home. Exactly what it was that kept us single-minded for so long is difficult to say. It just seemed logical that if we kept nibbling away at it, the boat would one day be fit to go to sea. That prospect alone was worth the effort but was it enough to sustain us for nearly a decade?

As the project entered its fifth year it became clear to us that there was more to it all. We were not only constructing a boat but a way of life that suited us. The demands felt stimulating, the value we attached to our labour genuine, and the constant challenges gave to each small success the feel of a triumph. Whatever price we might have to pay for such privileges, there was nothing else we would rather have been doing. Our training as crew mates was nearly over.

Whatever it was – whether we were compelled by a gathering set of circumstances, pride, stubbornness, a sense of obligation, or just because *Imago* was by now the expression of our spirit – we were halfway up the proverbial mountain ... we could not turn back.

Chapter 20

If you can meet with triumph and disaster, and treat these two impostors just the same... (Kipling)

We could not turn back...

'Who says so?' Fate, rising up, arms folded, very tall, looking down, stern faced. Fate, in a horribly belligerent mood, the planets well out of conjunction, an axial wobble to my star sign.

What do you do? 'What's the appropriate response? Obeisance, resistance, an acceptable human sacrifice? Do you beg, plead, repent, accept?

Bang! You are pregnant.

Bang! Your mother is dead.

Bang! Your beloved friend and mentor is dead.

Had I not changed from winter trousers to summer trousers, I might not have known for another month that I was pregnant. They were two inches too small, which was preposterous considering that neither of us carried more than sinew and bone connected by a thin coating of connective tissue. But when I looked in the mirror there was the slightly convex shape to the belly.

I didn't speak to anyone, but joined the sitting queue at the doctor's surgery next morning. 'Shopping,' I called out, 'see you at the boat-yard later.'

'You're five months pregnant,' the doctor beamed, 'a bit on the elderly side for a first child, but if you take care of yourself, with modern technology, you should be fine.'

'Ken, I'm pregnant.'
'But you won't be able to work!'

I'm on the wrong set – this is a different movie. She doesn't 'tell' him, she 'announces' it, with the dazzle of love in her eyes. He gathers her up, laughing, close to crying with the joy of it. She wards him off playfully, him contrite that he may have hugged 'them' too hard, sitting her down. She telling him not to fuss but loving it.

Wrong set, wrong movie. This is *Lawrence of Arabia* – alone in the vast desert.

For two days we lived as strangers. There was no anger about it, just scene after rolling scene: what yes to having a baby would mean, what no to having a baby would mean. It was not the sort of problem that could be debited and credited as a tidy list. My body yearned for a child, my mind counselled no. My history was against it, I might not be a good mother, I simply would not bring up a child alone, our lifestyle would be entirely different.

'I didn't mean it the way I said it.'

'I know you didn't,' I replied, not knowing ... not yet ... whether that was true.

'When you said you were pregnant I just felt jolted and scared. It would mean giving up the boat, perhaps losing you, things not being the same any more. I've imagined it though, designed a crib, seen it next to us by the bed. We could manage it if that's what you want. I'm sorry it came out like that, it's just that everything until then seemed so right. We'll have the baby if that's what you want.'

My decision then, and it proved to be the one I couldn't make, however much I agonised about it. If I could not decide, then we could not have a child. It was definitely not something to feel indecisive about.

Odd what comes to mind. I remembered a girlfriend being asked why she left her husband: 'Because he didn't beg me to stay.' I wondered whether the decision would have been different if Ken had played out that first scene. I don't believe so. I hope I wouldn't have been so impressionable as that. His reaction had been honest and truthful.

Twenty four hours of labour. My potential baby delivered into a stainless steel bowl, then taken away. Ken and I sadder and closer.

For many months the image of that clinical procedure haunted me. Every advertisement for nappies, wipes, gentle soaps, was a serrated knife in my heart. Suddenly every street corner, grass verge, front garden and porch was bursting with gurgling, suckling infants. The world was pink with babies, growing everywhere like plump, round mushrooms.

I would always wonder ... always know how old my child would have been this year. It is the price that women pay, in instalments, for ever.

The funeral for my mother was a quiet family affair. She had outlived all but one of her seven siblings as well as every friend she had ever known. It wasn't hard to let her go. I felt grateful that she had stayed with me for so long, time enough for her to know that I was happy and whole. Very early on the morning of the funeral I went for a long walk, down to the round pool (this time I had to climb a fence and trespass). Then across the meadows to the river, picking wild flowers and grasses as I went. The posy lay among the gaudy flowers reminding me of every spring we had shared together. Throughout the service I gazed at the coffin, visualised her, wondering how she lay, which dress she was wearing, were her hands placed over each other in the same way she had held them in life when she sat quietly at the end of the day?

*   *   *

The funeral for my friend was a very different affair. Hundreds of colleagues, friends, patients, ex-Borstal kids. Lords, professors, janitors, the long-serving postman. I was swamped and depressed. Separated, unable to find the space for my private grief. Struck down just before retirement, already planning for that atrium that would grow fabulous orchids. Talking about it only days before and me asking if I might buy the first in the collection. And now, placing that very first orchid on her grave.

For this person, especially, I would defy all these assaults: the only way to neutralise these terrible losses, until such time as I could convert them into the more peaceful realms of memory; indeed the only way to acknowledge each of their gifts was to get up, straighten my legs and continue walking.

When the snake eats the frog there is no malice in it.

Chapter 21

The bulk of the fitting out, excluding finishing touches such as fabrics, floor coverings, lights, instrumentation, pictures on the walls, was to take three more years.

Our methods by now were practised and familiar. Every day we sawed, planed, chiselled, jointed, glued and fixed. The air around us vibrated with proper boat-building sounds: the blunt notes of a sharp chisel, the high-pitched whine of jigsaw and router. Each handmade piece took on its own chunk of character, and the crowning moment, as a first coat of sealer declared the colour and grain of the wood, lost none of its appeal. Those first few months of fitting out were an immensely satisfying time.

The willow trees lining the gravel pits turned lime green, followed a few weeks later by suburban blossom trees hurrying into bloom. Instead of spring helping, as it tends to do, the project went into another serious decline. We were bemused by such a sudden loss of spirit.

There were three symptoms to the malady. First, the main goal, that of launching and sailing the boat, seemed stuck in reverse gear. The equation was precise: the longer we toiled, the further it slipped from our sights. Second, a lowering of productivity that even a 34-hour day could not have boosted. And third, the realisation that there is nothing so frustrating as absolute independence, which we may call, instead, poverty.

A meeting was called. We needed to take a very hard look at what was happening, find some remedies quickly. The conviction that we would eventually succeed, all the way, was no longer a matter of doubt, and so could not account for what was happening. Yet here were the first signs of a descent into reluctant labour. It would spoil it all. Even a corpuscle of resentment would tarnish the spirit of the project.

The explanation proved to be as simple as it was harsh – it was all the truth. With every piece of furniture in place, oak glowing, teak grain carefully matched, bunks ready to be slept in, even when we could boil the first kettle of water on the cooker, we would still only be halfway there.

The drain on our energy was real too. In June, Ken would be 48, I would be 42. We were pushing ourselves like 24-year-olds and wondering why expectations failed to match output. Inevitably some of the co-ordinating bits such as muscles, tendons, joints began to stage painful protests. Some days they all got together and went on strike!

The third problem, that of non-existent finance, was undoubtedly the most debilitating if only in its persistence. It had dogged us from the very beginning. Even Ken's knack of salvaging second-hand materials, of making existing objects serve another purpose, could not bail us out indefinitely.

The most obvious solution was to take full-time employment, perhaps even separate jobs – a depressing thought. When we sat down to estimate how much we needed to finish the boat then converted that sum into time, it was painfully clear that we might have to spend the next four years gazing wistfully at a half-finished boat. In other words, it would all be over. It was a heartbreaking dilemma.

'Stop it!' Was that me speaking in such vehement tones? Call yourself a counsellor? It was. Irritable and angry with it too.

'What the hell is the matter with us! Remember the oak tree, the mill, the engine, the chocolate-filled tubing? Who is to say that fate might not favour the foolish as well as the brave? It will all take longer, that's all!'

Meeting adjourned!

Our frugal lifestyle, born of necessity, now became a matter of Spartan survival. For the whole of that summer we lived mostly on eels or baked potatoes. On Sundays, 'special' baked potatoes, with cheese on top. Not that there is anything wrong with eels – very nourishing they are. Let us just say that neither of us would suffer withdrawal symptoms if we never saw or tasted one again.

Each dusk we collected half a dozen lob worms from the field next to the boat-yard then settled to fish patiently from the slipway. Supper might be 20 minutes later, four hours later or not at all. Tea bags had been used twice for a long time, now the teapot was stewed to make four bags last all day. Bread was the other staple – we ate it at every meal.

The supermarket chain of Budgens came to our rescue this time and it earned us the money for the paint. We joined as evening crew, stacking shelves for the next day's trade ... and we hated every minute of it.

Imagine returning to the worst aspects of school life: No talking! Stack them straight! Stand to attention when I talk to you! Call me Mister! As if the plain drudgery of it were not enough.

Ken approached it all with his usual enthusiasm. Being a big lad, he was put on the pet foods. He soon devised a method of packing the shelves solid, with lightning speed, leaving him time over to help the largely middle-aged women who found some of the heavy cartons difficult to handle.

The deputy manager, an anxious, Dickensian sort of chap, only put on this earth to complain, gave Ken a dressing down. One of his tins was only showing half its label. A very serious misdemeanour indeed since this particular canine delicacy was 'new and improved!'

I hid behind the nearest box of Bonio while the hero in my life got his telling off. What I longed to do was open a box and bite hard on one of the bone shaped biscuits to stifle my giggles. My disrespect was noticed and I think I only escaped instant dismissal because, guess what, staff were hard to get! The man seemed to view enthusiasm of any kind as an assault on his personal authority. After that, Ken's work became as perfunctory as everyone eise's.

But it was at Budgens that we met Melody, a tiny woman with an enormous heart – big enough to tuck not only us but also a whole campful of refugees under her wings. Long after we left the job, she would visit us at the yard, bringing her two young boys with her. Stowed inside her bottomless 'morning at the boat-yard' bag there would always be enough sandwiches and cake for five boys.

That summer in spite of, and because of, Budgens, we shot-blasted the outside of the boat and painted her. The blasting was every bit as gruelling as the first time, but after stacking shelves we were never again to describe any task as 'tedious', besides, it was the prospect of seeing *Imago* in paint that provided the energy. We hand brushed each of the first seven coats, rubbing down lightly before the last, which Ken sprayed on to give a mirror finish.

We worked every day of that summer, only stopping when the light faded and it was time to fish for supper. This was the last of the really big jobs and the most spectacular. It really did seem that she had only to set her canvas wings to make the metaphor complete: dull brown nymph into dragonfly.

We chose a deep green for the hull. Not a wholly sensible choice for the tropics, perhaps, but it was a colour that suited her traditional lines. Apart from the handrails, tabernacles and window frames, picked out in the same green, the superstructure was white. We stood back to admire her. She was all we could have hoped for.

Sometimes, when there were separate jobs to be done, we hardly saw each other though the distance between us might only be a matter of yards. There were days we didn't speak at all until it was time to pack up the tools. These carefree silences were occasionally broken by a game we played. It had started after the painting.

'I'm going over to that rock pool again tonight.'

'Oh ... we're not weighing anchor today then?'

'No hurry, it's nice here, I'll catch some shrimp from the pool – we'll have them for supper.'

Even back at the caravan before going to bed:
'It's your watch.'
'You crook! I did the last two to six.'
'I'm the skipper.'
In all these day-dreams the sea sparkled in bright sunlight ...
Imago lay quietly at anchor ... warm water swished gently along
her hull.

As we reached what is always the most expensive phase in boat-
building, Ken was confronted by some of the most satisfying
challenges to his mechanical ingenuity. Using various diameters
of scrap stainless steel tubing and plate, he constructed the wheel
and pedestal for £28. A true circle was obtained with a borrowed
plumbers pipe bender and a highly sophisticated jig comprising
a circle of six inch nails!

We bought the basic elements of Morse controls for the engine
only to suffer a severe disappointment. Having taken every care
to use only stainless or bronze metals in the vicinity of the cockpit
in order to avoid excessive compass deviation, we now discovered
that all the working parts in the controls were made of mild
(magnetic) steel. Ken had been quite prepared to make the boxing
to house the controls, but now he also had to spend ten painstaking
evenings in the shed making exact replicas of each small moving
component in stainless steel.

Although the compass can be corrected for the sometimes
dramatic deviation on a steel boat, it did seem pointless to construct
a non-magnetic pedestal assembly only to find that the Morse
controls, just inches from the compass position, were magnetic.

Having recovered our equilibrium, so to speak, Ken concentrated
on the final adjustments in the engine room. Several evenings in
the shed resulted in the heat exchanger and the header tank,
followed shortly afterwards by the manifold that he had made
from round barrel and box section.

One day, people would pass by the boat and stop for a chat.

By and by, Ken might tell them that he had built his boat, but no one would ever fully understand quite what that meant.

I concentrated on the hatches. Aircraft perspex again – this time it was a windscreen, a full inch thick. The forward hatch was framed in steel to withstand big seas that might come aboard at that point. A rugged vessel is what counts when conditions are at their most challenging and *Imago* had that business look about her.

Another bitterly cold winter. We resorted to scrounging offcuts from every boat in the yard to keep the solid fuel fire going in the caravan. For two weeks, at the beginning of December, drifting snow forced us into hibernation. Things began to look pretty desperate. Keeping the fire alive became as much an obsession to us as it must have been to Neanderthal man. I bought in dried beans, lentils and peas – a gallon of soup a day was our staple diet.

Funds were low, spirits were low, we should give up, be sensible, admit defeat. We were still years away from a sailing yacht. How much harder will it get? We both need to have our heads examined!

'We'll launch her on the next flood water!'

I looked at him in amazement. But he was right. What we needed now were real deadlines. A vague time in the future was eroding our confidence. We would finish her in the water.

Chapter 22

Imago was probably the largest boat ever built in Shepperton. She was certainly the largest ever to be launched from a slipway normally used by dinghies and small river cruisers. Even before laying the keel, Ken had stood at the top of the slope to figure out the logistics of it all. On that same day he had also determined that he would launch her himself.

The cost of hiring a low loader and crane was not really prohibitive at about £200 but to have built her with his own hands and then have to rely on assistance, on this of all days? Downright unethical!

The axle we had stumbled across on the day I had been called a 'poor little blighter,' the one Ken had said he 'might' use, was always the one he'd been determined to use.

My faith wavered at this point. Thoughts dwelled heavily on squashed buildings, *Imago* lying on her side causing an obstruction on the main thoroughfare. I bit my nails to the quick first, then decided to knit some blanket squares to keep my mind off the word 'catastrophe'. Not a bright solution since blankets are closely associated with first aid.

Both axles were made ready for their short-lived, if illustrious, part in the proceedings. Design testing proved simple, jack up the boat, all 20 tons, let the weight sit on them for a couple of weeks, then check for stress. The truck tyres stood up well but the original tyres on the bomb trailer promptly burst. After a half-hearted search for replacements, we spent a day welding short lengths of scaffold tube around the hubs – she would go to the launch on what looked like a pair of Gatling guns.

We alerted those who had watched over us since the day the

keel was laid, six years before. Foremost among those who had kept faith with us were Ken's own family, in particular his sister Fay and her husband John. They not only visited every three or four months but also brought with them a sparkling enthusiasm about all that we were trying to do. Fay would stroke the wood, peer into the bilges, listen patiently as Ken went into too much technical detail, always pronounced that everything we had done was wonderful. Had we only added one more screw since her last visit she would have noticed it. She was a tonic. Sometimes we even found ourselves waiting on her next visit to give us a boost. She was a noticeable woman, built as large as Ken and just as restless, angry and capable.

I suggested to Ken that his mother Beatrice do the honours with a bottle of Spumante. It just might be that she would rise to something so obvious – might even say well done!

It rained steadily for more than a week. The river began to fill and flood. It looked increasingly as though the launch would take place six years to the day from when the keel was laid. And so it was!

The slow haul began on the Friday morning. An amber flood alert for the Thames Valley had already been issued. We planned to move her to a position where she was poised on the slipway, before calling in our witnesses. They were advised to bring 'interesting' flasks and large hankies.

A three to one reduction pull from the boat-yard truck ... *Imago* lurched reluctantly from her birthplace. All the tyres promptly sank to their hubs in the Surrey gravel. She had moved two feet.

This was to be the pattern of progress for all of the hundred and fifty yards to the slipway: jack her up, set down steel plate to spread the load, haul again ... another two feet. Each time she swayed and groaned under her great weight like an elderly, overweight duck.

By six o'clock that night the trolley had travelled 50 yards to solid ground between the boat-yard buildings. The rest of the journey, through the gates and round onto the road towards the slipway promised to be easier. By then it was pitch black and bitterly cold. We opted to spend the night aboard. By lunchtime the next day, *Imago* would hopefully be floating in the Thames.

I rang Fay and Richard and Mick.

'This is the call' – the agreed code phrase for launch day. The final tow would begin at 8am.

Some time during the night it started to snow. By dawn it lay two inches thick on the ground. A possibility that we had not considered, but there was no moving the boat back now. The river was as high as it was likely to be for the rest of the year. The launch MUST go ahead.

Paralysingly cold. The temperature had plummeted to minus eight degrees: almost too cold to breathe in. We should all have been lying sleepwarm in our beds or huddled close to a living-room fire with coffee and the morning papers. A day to be looked at through a pane of glass – beautiful, in a desolate sort of way.

Our foul-weather friends stuck with us, in appalling conditions, for the whole of the day. Apart from shovelling snow and laying down steel plates there was little else for them to do but wait and watch as *Imago* made her tortuous way to the slipway.

By lunchtime the cold had penetrated to the bone. After that the numbness that precedes hypothermia made it bearable so long as you stayed rooted to the spot. *Imago* ploughed her way through an honour guard of snowmen and women.

At 5pm, in failing light, the special few seconds at last seemed imminent. The skeg was now poised an inch from the water. All that held her back was the steel cable that ran from the boat-yard winch at the top of the slope to the bow. Ken's mother was handed the bottle of Spumante to sprinkle over the bow...

And then it happened! Just then – just as we were about to savour the spectacle of a proper dignified launch, the concrete slipway suddenly cracked under both axles. *Imago* sank slowly into the ground.

* * *

Everything that happened next has been retold countless times from a dozen different points of view, according to who was standing where on the day.

'Do you remember the day we launched *Imago*?' The cold, the noise, the confusion, a near drowning, your mother's prayers, the relief, the joy!

The winch cable snapped free from its pulley. The shock of its release cannoned the two axles together which in turn catapulted *Imago* towards the river at accelerating miles an hour. All but one of the restraining ropes parted like strands of cotton wool as she left.

Total, frozen shock!

Ken's mother, open mouthed, holding the bottle aloft, a bystander, thinking it was the planned moment, raising a solo cheer, wide eyes gazing at lengths of frayed rope dangling limply in their hands.

Heroically, but forlornly, Ken tried to hang on to the remaining rope. He was pulled forward into a stumbling run. He stood waist high in the river before he let it go. The spiralling winch cable zipped wildly through a dozen pairs of legs before it was spotted by Fay. Big girl – big voice.

'Grab the cable!'

With remarkable synchronisation born of panic, 24 hands snatched at the cable and *Imago* was hauled in faster than she had gone out. The rudder had swung. Instead of returning to the slipway, she veered round and headed towards the line of moored boats. Ken rushed over to fend her off. As he ran along the narrow deck of the threatened vessel he slipped on the ice, plunged into the river ... and disappeared!

By then other people had gained control over *Imago* and eased off from pulling. The only person who saw Ken fall into the river was his mother Beatrice. She began to pray.

'Please God, please don't let my Kenny drown!

Ken heard her as he went under. As his feet touched the mud he realised instantly that with a flood current running he only had one chance. He bent his knees, pushed hard and up he shot – straight from the water to land in exactly the same spot on the boat from where he had fallen. His mother was still praying … 'Don't let my Kenny drown.'

Exhausted, wet to the skin, desperately cold, and still a happy man. Now we all cheered!

Varying degrees of shock and exposure were treated medicinally with volatile liquids and a noisy debriefing. Ken was taken into the boat-yard office where he was stripped of his wet clothing with the calm efficiency and detachment most women have when responding to crises. The ribald comments came later after he emerged dressed in a smaller man's clothing. We all hooted with laughter. That warmed us all up nicely.

I'll launch her myself, he had said, so we had all seen it through with him. I do try to be angry with him sometimes for testing his friendships so.

Imago lay snugly at her first berth and exactly true at all points on the water-line. How splendid she looked – not so much sitting on the water as embracing it. We were numb with pleasure and relief.

It seemed a casual enough gesture. He simply handed me a small key.

'Start her up, love!…'

That he should give that moment to me! I doubt if any woman has felt so emotional about an engine starting up for the first time.

As it does, of course … every time … first time.

Chapter 23

From every conceivable point of view it should have been a catastrophe, with dead bodies to prove it. Launching away in such dramatic style endeared *Imago* to everyone present. She had sat out in the middle of the swollen river for a long moment, her weight holding her against the flood, as if to say, 'Well? What do you think?'

It might still be a long way from sailing trials with Ken as skipper, but here was the first glimpse of the finishing line. Exactly the encouragement we needed.

Most of the rest could now be labelled finishing work, and of the large tasks there remained only one – the making of the masts. We really were naive enough to think that.

Ken's mother was deeply disappointed that *Imago* had avoided her naming ceremony. What with her prayers having saved her son from drowning, she felt morbidly convinced that unless the ritual was properly observed a shadow would be cast over the future. We, too, felt that naming one's vessel is an important psychological event. And so it was agreed that we should all gather again in the summer at the place called Runnymede and do the thing again.

Another deadline spurred us on. The next objective was to consolidate the interior so that we could move in and live aboard as well as make her presentable for Naming Day.

As fate would yet again have it, we were fortunate in getting to know a professional upholsterer who was working on his boat in the yard. He generously talked us through the basics of making soft furnishings. Several months before, we had acquired a second-hand sail-maker's sewing machine. The foam for the swabs came from salvaged shop furniture, which we trimmed to size before glueing the layers together. We spent the very last of our remaining funds on the material: Rexine for the bunk swabs and the seating around the table; heavy Dralon for the lounging seats. After the usual period of fretting and worrying because we literally could not afford to make mistakes, checking the measurements a dozen times more, we made the first anxious cut with the wallpaper scissors. It really was easier than it looked – we even raised our ambitions by setting buttons into the backs of the seating to give them a look of substance and professionalism.

Just as the paint had joined up the outside of the boat, the cushions and flooring did the same for the inside: enhancing the woodwork, turning a sketch into a framed picture.

The main saloon is exceptionally large for a 40-footer due to the exaggerated beam of the 'Spray'. It allowed for a division of the space into three distinct areas for eating, cooking and relaxing. A triple cluster of spotlights attached to the main mast support accentuated this separation. With the galley and table lighting off, someone reading in the lounging area could feel relaxed and private, while a single light directed at the table lent atmosphere and intimacy to special meals.

Between concentrating on the maze of wiring that had to run from the batteries to the lights, gauges, electronic equipment (if we ever acquired some), bilge pumps, water supply and shower, Ken indulged my home-making instincts.

Each one of the individual pieces he made for our home was as romantic as roses on a breakfast tray. After all the physical, often dirty, work, these homely touches afforded me real pleasure. A cabinet for the saloon bulkhead, a desk for me to write letters at and resurrect my writing hobby, all carved by hand. This from a man who has never once bought me a birthday or Christmas card or a spontaneous gift. A man who communicates his feelings through his labours, who means what he does.

A few weeks later, when the weather relented, Richard came with us on our very first trip up the river ... a taste of what was to be: the slow thrug of the diesel engine vibrating gently through the cockpit floor; an easy turn on the wheel to point her bow, and we were on the move.

No more a yacht, as yet, than a nymph is to a dragonfly, but nothing in the future would quite compare with that first slow cruise up the river and back again. Bulky as she was, everything about her in the water was graceful, unhurried.

I watched Ken as he stood where the main mast would be, saw him sigh deeply, the fretting and the toil set aside. Just briefly he could abandon himself to a sense of wholesome satisfaction. I knew that he was deeply moved.

We exchanged a look, registered each other's feelings. For the next hour, as we glided past willow trees, riverside homes, and pasture, the future rolled around inside our minds.

How would she handle in big seas? Could we do her justice? What is courage? How will the fear strike? Shall we really see whales? The whole wide-screen panorama of dawns and sunsets – just the three of us on the vast oceans. Soon enough now we would have the answers.

The summer of 1985 proved to be one of the wettest on record. During the month of June it rained every day, except that on the 21st, when Ken celebrated his 49th birthday and *Imago* was named, the downpour held off until the evening.

We had journeyed downriver to Runnymede the day before. Six hours at the helm in rain so dense and straight it was hard to tell whether it was falling from the sky or rising up from the ground. It was bitterly disappointing, having worked so hard since the launch and invited so many friends to celebrate with us though we knew our families would make it, whatever the conditions. Fay would be striding across the field next morning in her sou'wester and galoshes to make sure there was a proper, if rather low-key, ceremony.

The chosen mooring lay opposite the Kennedy memorial, that

small yet dignified pagoda set against a hill to commemorate, in a peculiarly poignant way, the desolation that followed President Kennedy's death when a universal feeling of hope was ended so abruptly, so brutally. Runnymede, a site in England that is as famous as Stonehenge: the place where the Magna Carta was signed and a site that has remained designated common ground ever since.

After deciding to be philosophical about the weather we went to bed.

'After all,' I reasoned, 'nothing could be worse than the conditions we all endured on launch day, at least this is warm rain!'

It was decided that we should all try to enjoy ourselves in the perverse way that the English have of defying their climate.

Having shrugged our shoulders about it all, we were not even surprised to find, next morning, that the sun was there, cast high above the horizon in a cloudless azure sky; nor to be told later that it continued to rain on most of the English counties except Berkshire. Providence again.

Our friends and family came to us. By late morning the bankside was dotted with moving flowers, more than a hundred people, all dressed in happy boat-naming colours, setting up for picnics: not so much a garden party as a herbaceous border. A heart-warming sight to take with us wherever we would go.

This could be nowhere else but England on a summer's day: dogs, children, painted sunshades, tables and chairs, fishermen and ducks, florid overweight cricketers guarding a single stump, butterflies and ox-eye daisies.

At three in the afternoon on 21 June 1985 ... 'I name this yacht *Imago* ... and all who sail in her.'

'Who'd like a trip up the river?' called Ken.

An extraordinary sight to crown the day. *Imago* thundering downstream with 57 passengers aboard, low as a raft in the water, only the bunting waving from the two posts stuck in the tabernacles showing above a pyramid of bodies that covered every square inch of the superstructure.

A memorable day.

Another six hours of torrential rain and we were back at our mooring in Shepperton, still dazed by the warmth of the occasion. All that faith: we felt a broadening sense of responsibility about preserving it.

No money. Still, such a lot to be done. Yet it cannot end here ... the promise has been spread wide now.

A few days later we towed the caravan to the far side of the cricket club and set light to it. None of the members came down to the boat-yard to see what Ken was about. After twelve years opinions about him had not been raised much above or beyond 'handyman'. If Ken felt any disappointment he did not show it. He simply left.

Chapter 24

For me, living aboard was returning home to the river. We packed our few belongings away then rested for a while, fishing and chatting, getting the feel of our new environment, finding it altogether the life we wanted to lead. Until we became too old to climb the companionway steps, *Imago* would be our home. When the time came, Ken was certain he would beach her somewhere and cut a doorway into the hull.

Although *Imago* was charged with a spirit that seems to emanate from things that are fashioned by hand, she was never an obsession, nor, in some abstract way, did we even possess her. There was something about love in that. Had we allowed the boat to become indispensable, the courage to sail her would have been very hard to find. She was a vehicle to enhance the quality of our lives together. If she were lost it must not mean that we too were lost – if it did then we had got it wrong. That is not to say *Imago* is not a well-loved boat, only that possessions do not feed the soul.

The final stages. Yet another make or break situation. A full set of basic electronic equipment would cost more than we had already spent on the project and a thousand pounds was the lowest quote on just the bare wood to make the masts. Where were we to find even a hundred pounds? Too much of a worry altogether so Ken hauled out a long baulk of timber, left in a ditch by a roadside gang a few years before. It became the bowsprit.

Once again we were becalmed. Would anyone sponsor two crazy but well-intentioned people who want, more than anything else, to see the world with their own eyes, report back, confirm how wonderful it is, make a sound case for better conservation, who are desperately trying to earn that privilege by building the means to get there? We were too shy to even ask.

The problems we still faced were immense: masts, rigging, batteries, sails, food, a radio, a tender, anchors, warps, fuel, shackles, winches, charts ... the list went over the page.

Frustration was a constant ache inside us. We still possessed the energy and the will but if the months slipped by, as they were doing, if we had to stop altogether, how would we ever find the strength to see it through?

Nevertheless, there was much to enjoy about living on the river. Watching boats disgorge from the lock was a favourite occupation. Hired cruisers rushed out at high speed leaving a huge wake astern of them; their three-point turns with engines racing, the highway manoeuvres of car drivers on holiday. Occasionally an old barge would slide majestically from the lock, a deep throated chug echoing from the banks: the sound of an engine working at the slow pace of the river; one piston stroke a second, for anything up to a hundred years.

It was only our second night aboard when Ken fell into the river. Skipper of his own vessel he might be, but there wasn't much dignity about it. Someone had given us an old bicycle to use for shopping. We decided it should be brought aboard each night. I was down below knitting away some of the worry when the boat started to rock. I presumed it was a larger than usual bow wave from one of the hire boats. No point in going up on deck to ask them to slow down – they would be well past by now – might as well finish this row and then see what the rogue vessel looked like before it reached the bend.

A minute or so later I climbed into the cockpit for a leisurely look. The river was as calm as a ceramic tile. Odd. Turning towards the bank I saw Ken standing on the pontoon close by the boat. There was something different about his posture – a stiffness. Then I noticed water dripping from his cuffs.

'You're wet!'

'I am.'

'Where's the bike?'

Ken pointed at the water.

Although it was not the story I told to the rest of the boat-yard next day, the true version was quite plausible. As Ken walked the bike towards the boat, a passer-by called out to him, wanting to know the whereabouts of another boat. In swivelling around to answer, Ken's foot caught against one of the mooring cleats. As he tripped he ran, as he ran the bike swerved to port, he to starboard. Both plunged into the water at the same moment from opposite sides of the pontoon. As we prodded about for the bicycle with the boat-hook, we laughed till it hurt, even harder when we found we had caught a fish in the spokes of the back wheel!

But *Imago* was built for the sea. Despite the fun, the gentle pace, the novelty of the environment, we found the lack of progress increasingly irksome. We painted a house, Ken overhauled some engines, I did occasional welding with a small engineering firm but it was only enough to pay for the mooring and to keep us in potatoes.

Just when it seemed that the bubble of frustration inside us would finally burst, events took a spectacular turn. We always wondered why it always waited until our spirits had sunk to boot level.

Concrete floors this time. Peter Turner was branching out again, into agricultural technology. He had acquired the patents for a revolutionary grain-drying floor. Our task was to travel around England supervising the laying of them.

We helped in the construction of 16 floors as far away as Northampton and Essex. It was punishing labour, setting up heavy concrete sections, bolting them together, blowing up long sausages of plastic hosing with compressors, trowelling smooth tons of quick-setting concrete slurry. Seven in the morning until eight in the evening for three or four days in a row, then immediately on to the next site. Every stroke with the trowel earned us a millimetre of mast. We slaved at it.

Galvanised wire, bottle screws, batteries, marine radio, shackles, pulleys ... crossing them off the list with a thick red pen. Enough money left over for one mast. Three months previously there'd been barely sufficient in the kitty for five pounds of potatoes. Such was the ebb and flow of our finances.

The mizzen-mast is special. It's 'Bill's mast'. William Roberts – friend extraordinaire. He came down from Worcester to visit us while we were debating whether to go ahead with the single mast or hang on a bit longer to see if we could raise all of the £760 for the two. Bill was my closest personal friend. I was 25 when he fell in love with me. It broke his heart when I said no to his proposal but we remained friends and were fiercely protective of each other. Three days after his visit a cheque arrived through the post for £400. The terms were couched in such a way that we could accept without embarrassment of any sort.

'I am so certain that you will make it, and that you deserve to, that I enclose a down payment for my first holiday with you, at a destination of your choice.'

Knee deep in chippings, intoxicated by the resinous scent of Norwegian spruce, we routed the timber to hollow the masts, scarfed the massive joints and glued together the 20-foot lengths of timber. We thought only of the following spring. Nothing now stood between *Imago* and her date with the Thames Estuary, even if we had to tie bed sheets to the poles!

Mast Day. Another celebration. And another bitterly cold day since it was February again of the eighth year. A few days before, with the help of our friends from the boat-yard, we manhandled the masts down to the boat, where they were hauled up using a ten-foot lever, a block and tackle and the winch.

Imago was totally transformed. There is only one word that fits – majestic!

That evening we walked over to the lock to gaze back at the masts. Ever since that moment it has been hard to believe that what we were seeing was anything more than just a dream in

Ken's head. We had not built the yacht that lay there. We couldn't have done!

The masts were decorated with bunting and fairy lights. Melody made us a boat-shaped cake. Let's all go together, now, tonight. Thank you, dear friends, we would not be here today without you all. Keep faith with us ... just a little longer.

'Yes, sir, we can make you a basic set of sails.'

'How much did you say?'

'It's difficult to be precise, sir, but you will find our estimate most competitive.'

'How much?'

'Only £2,300!'

Chapter 25

Two thousand pounds was so ludicrous a sum that far from depressing our spirits we simply looked at each other with wry humour.

So, the last gate was locked and barred? Well, so much the better: it was not the first obstacle to be tunnelled under, climbed over, wriggled through; what of those others that mysteriously disappeared as we approached them?

It is the same with any venture. It need not be a boat but any labour you set your heart on. Once the path is chosen it is only the trying that matters and neither man, beast, nor circumstance can keep you from it.

Unfortunately the 'make what you cannot afford' principle could not serve us this time. Such relatively small quantities of cloth, together with yarn, cordage, eyelets, needles and leather, left only a token difference in price. The logistics were also a problem – where to find a large enough area to lay out the material for cutting and making up.

Finally we decided on the best second-hand sails that we could afford, making alterations where necessary to suit our rig. With the basic four sails we could take her to sea.

No two people ever went out to find work with more enthusiasm. Ken was taken on by a local transport firm. Within weeks he became their fitter and carpenter as well as driving the heavy goods vehicles. With his single-minded knack of transferring his loyalty completely from one environment to another, always amiable and willing, they took to him, as he did to them.

I took a job washing up at the nearest hotel in Shepperton, five hours a day, seven days a week. It was the first time we had been separated for work. The saloon was crammed with talk when we met up at the end of each day, though not about driving from here to there or washing pots and pans. It was as if we no longer inhabited the world of today, as if we had lived in a time warp for the last eight years. The things that went on! A man could earn £200 a week! It was nothing, it seemed, to spend £80 on a single item of clothing, even an ordinary person would entertain a debt of several thousand pounds! It brought home to us as forcefully as culture shock that on an income like that we could live in great style had we wanted to.

Is it possible, then, to escape the greedy clutches of the twentieth century? I only know that we felt not a moment of envy in all of the eight years for holidays, cinema, dining out, gadgets, fashion, videos, potions or palliatives. If I missed anything at all it was the pleasures of hospitality. We could not lay on a good table for our friends, though I do not think we lost a single one because of it.

What we did have was endless variation, fun and sadness in equal measure, together with some of the physical and mental preparation needed to cope with the discomfort and constraints of travelling by sea on a pittance of money.

About then, something happened that was to serve us well and serve us ill. A momentum built up: an irresistible quickening of pace, of things coming together. As we raised up our glasses to the new year of 1987 we realised that this was the year when we would take *Imago* to sea.

Both the transport firm and the hotel knew of our plans and their kindness was overwhelming. Sponsorship might be the current mode of setting up for adventures but everyone around us made whatever contribution they could, with the utmost discretion, to help us on our way. Real sponsorship, a matter of heart and mind, not profit.

Every Sunday I was sent home from the Anchor Hotel with

two roast dinners 'to fatten us up a bit'. At cost price, they provided the food for our eve of departure 'thank you' party. On top of all that, they relieved me of the tedium of my job with so much warmth and encouragement that I day-dreamed happily into the suds – each pan to scour, another square inch of sail.

Melody took to having picnics with us at least twice a week.

'I seem to have packed more than we needed.' She said this every time as she shared out the cake and delicious homemade goodies, 'leaving behind' a tin of cake or biscuits from each trip.

Ken's firm gave him several lengths of stainless steel tubing, left there years before from an undelivered load. These became the stanchions for the guard-rail around the boat.

'We're having a clear out, Ken, take anything that you can see a use for.'

We were given a sea toilet from one of the boats in the yard, brand new, not even fitted, and never a price mentioned. An anchor from another: 'Too big for mine,' was the excuse. Two small winches for hauling in sail, a large quantity of rope suitable as mooring lines, cable for navigation lights, a mascot. All donated to us.

Not one of these gestures passed us by, nor would we forget them, wherever we might find ourselves in the future.

The first sail came by post from a sail exchange agency. A highly prestigious make, in excellent condition. This, the mainsail, cost £325 – the foresails would be less expensive.

As soon as we had saved enough money for the mizzen-sail, we set a date for the journey downriver – 21 June 1987. To be truthful we ran out of steam. Another year at the yard earning money would have paid for a bit more sophistication where rigging and navigation equipment were concerned, but another year at that time wasn't in us.

Not that we underestimated the value of life raft or inflatable, flares, safety harnesses, flags, life-jackets, or waterproof gear, but what we needed even more were the larger winches, running track for the booms, reefing ties, self steering, jam cleats – gear that would assist in the handling of the vessel. If we had sailed before, even as a pastime, we might have managed well enough, but nothing would compensate for our lack of experience without the assistance of adequate running gear.

The feeling that we must make a start on our journey overwhelmed us. We might chase after all the equipment needed and still not get to the end of it. We thought of Joshua Slocum sailing the first 'Spray', with his one-handed chronometer, blocks and tackle, his two simple navigation aids: the sextant and instinct. We also knew that it was the wealth and breadth of his experience that served him best.

It was too late for us to understand the art of seamanship, indeed we held it in awe, but we both had good listening ears coupled with a student's appetite for learning from sound tutors. Reading up was a sight more difficult, even about basic techniques. The textbook jargon was baffling since mariners tend to find six different terms that describe the same piece of gear: the longer the history of a subject, the stranger the language becomes.

Barely a week before the journey downriver, I drove to Southampton with the £250 we had saved and bought the foresails. They were slightly smaller than the sail plans suggested but it was too late to alter them. They were strong and in good condition, which mattered more. We chose strong, heavy sails suitable for a heavy displacement yacht that tends to slug it out rather than do a lively dance. In light breezes she would always be at a disadvantage compared with the modern slimline yachts, but in rough conditions she would show up well and need the heavier sails.

The first few weeks of June were frenetic: we must either begin our journey or take a holiday! Provisions to plan and stow away; friends from further afield to visit – perhaps the last time for many years – spring cleaning inside and out; arrangements to be made for the last gathering, a few days before leaving. Dozens, too, of those small but time-consuming jobs such as fixing the navigation lights, making a cradle to support the masts while we negotiated the bridges.

In those final weeks so much kindness was bestowed on us that we thought our hearts would burst. No one had a thought to stop us going, least of all ourselves, yet it is so much harder as one gets older, to leave friends. Our feelings were buffeted about, each emotion at war with the other. Deep down, excitement about what may lie ahead; profound sadness about leaving the warm bosom of support that had so helped to bring it all about – an uncomfortable mix.

The 'thank you' party was another picnic sort of day. The chef from the Anchor Hotel used his ovens to bake vol-au-vents and sausages; Melody made the cake in the shape of our vessel. As we raised the sails for a preview, a cheer went up that must have reached as far as Shepperton High Street.

Our local newspaper, *The Surrey Herald*, took photographs and wrote up a charming account of the project. I wrote to Prince Charles: he had spoken in recent years about matters that deeply concerned us, in particular about conservation and the need to eliminate prejudice. We admired both his views and his courage in declaring them. For us he was always the man who should be king, someone interested in youth development, art, culture, comparative religions, architecture, conservation. We admired his refusal to accept the lowest common denominator and wondered why the British press lampooned him so. A man who 'talked' to plants? Yes every time to a man who regards the living world in that way. We imagined his discomfort when he was persuaded to attend pop concerts and wondered, even then, whether such a mismatched union with Diana could survive.

I felt he would both understand and approve of what we had set out to do. Would he acknowledge Ken's achievement by authorising the lifting of Tower Bridge, please? The letter from Kensington Palace was polite and indifferent. A secretary passed on 'His Highness' Best Wishes.' It left me feeling embarrassed about having written at all. Laurens van der Post was second choice but I did not write a letter!

Yet it was something I dearly wanted for Ken. Richard Branson rushed across the Atlantic weighed down with sponsor's labels. We watched on television as he passed under the 'Bridge of Britain' in triumph. I felt that Ken had done just as well, given the disparity of circumstances, and besides, he was a London man!

Ken's sister Fay made it happen. Her direct approach was the better one. First she rang the BBC, putting her case rather bluntly:

'Never mind all the carnage and doom you people put out. There are things going on in this country that you never even look for. Just you get down to Shepperton in Middlesex. There is a man down there who has built a yacht with his bare hands from nothing. And he's going to sail it around the world!'

Come they did, decided to film us for a day, which was a great commotion one way and another. Short snatches of film and stage-managed interviews, but when put together for the local news the professionalism showed in a delightful ten-minute sequence, which appeared a few days later.

More exciting by far, where we were concerned, the director of outside broadcasts picked up the comment about Tower Bridge and approached the bridge master. No doubt she felt it would make a nice bit of film should they choose to broaden their interest in us at some future date.

No other gesture could say 'well done' so completely and emphatically as this, no other photograph in our collection would be treasured more. At 3.45pm 29 June 1987, Tower Bridge would be raised for a small unknown yacht called *Imago*.

Perhaps I was the only one who thought it was the least they could do!

Chapter 26

We very nearly missed our rendezvous with Tower Bridge.

Ken was halfway up the mizzen-mast, tying on a cable, when it fell. Onlookers say that it bounced like a springboard after first hitting the pulpit rail then the traffic bollard at the top of the bank. They also said that the look of horror on Ken's face lasted all the way from vertical to the moment he disappeared into the river, still sitting in his bosun's chair.

No one moved. A stream of bubbles marked his entry point. Several seconds later Ken's face appeared from the Thames looking totally bemused. All too much for the men aboard who could see by then that the mast had suffered no serious damage other than a few superficial gashes in the paintwork. Somebody chuckled. That was the cue for every male present to dissolve into hysterical laughter, Ken included.

At the sound of the crashing woodwork, I leaped out on deck to be greeted by a world gone crazy. Ken in the river gurgling his silly head off, every man from the yard hanging on to the boat like chimpanzees, rolling and staggering, clutching at each other in the greatest glee, the mast still bouncing on the pulpit.

I know it was simply an outburst of relief, that if the mast had fractured they would have closed ranks around their friend, but at the time I could not see the funny side – only the prospect of having to make another mast and missing our date with the bridge.

Ken was hauled on deck. His fast entry into the water, pile driven as he was by the weight of the falling mast, had forced two feet of mud up both trouser legs. Pounds of evil smelling sludge poured from his waistline.

There was much ribald comment about the humiliating effects

of fear. It did look comical. I laughed then but it was a nasty shock that could have spoiled everything.

Richard patted the stem of *Imago* before pushing her away from the mooring. The feelings about our final departure were reflected in the slowly waving hands from the small huddle of friends and family left behind on the bank. Our own feelings went out from the boat towards them ... until we rounded the long bend and were finally out of sight.

After the hectic pace of the last few weeks we felt tired. No time to think, let alone savour the fact that a dream might be coming true. Even for the best of reasons, goodbyes are always sad. In the first few hours we hardly spoke. Ken was anxious – almost irritable. I wanted to shout:

'Stop! Hold on a minute! Let's start this again, we should be happy.'

Instead, we were filled with a sense of enormity, of a calling to account. Building the boat was barely half of the challenge we had set ourselves and now we felt as uncertain and vulnerable as a pair of adolescents leaving home.

We taped the *London A to Z* onto the hatch cover, together with the list of bridges, heights, tide times. Our first 'chart'.

Approaching Sunbury railway bridge we heard a shout. There was Margaret, the housekeeper from the hotel, she and her husband waving frantically from the bridge. They had chased after us in their car, determined to see us off. A mile further on and they were there again, this time on the towpath. What pleasure such gestures bring. My spirits rose by several degrees.

Our friends on the bank; David, the chef, feeding the ducks; Fay organising the deck cargo; Margaret's final wave: these were the vivid images we would remember from the day *Imago* left her yard of origin.

* * *

Thirty-five other bridges to negotiate before our special date with Tower Bridge. With the masts lowered we were about 15 feet above water level. If our calculations were correct, all the road and rail bridges could be negotiated safely, though some, especially Hammersmith, are only passable at low tide. In the event, it was only the third railway bridge that troubled us, understandably so since, unaccountably, it was missing from our list. I aimed for the middle then closed my eyes.

'Ten inches to spare,' said Ken. I know he lied to spare me.

The first stopover was at Molesey Lock. We were soon in bed after dining well on a tin of game stew provided by Margaret. Next morning we enjoyed a smooth run to Teddington and the beginning of the tidal waterway. Gliding along as we were with the engine throbbing gently at tickover speed, the wildlife ignored our passage. We photographed a heron sitting impassively only yards away and exchanged a smile. After all, wasn't this the main reason behind our labours? Things were looking better. We began to relax a little.

At Kew, on the following evening, we found room on the towpath. After the steady, flowing rhythms of engine and passing landscape, the sense of being joined with the inexorable movement of a great sea-bound river, cars and people alike seemed altogether too fast and aggressive.

London at last. City of bridges. A passage through the city by river was always part of the dream and we savoured it. Under Hammersmith with two feet to spare, then finally, and it felt like weeks, we came within sight of Tower Bridge.

We tied up at a barge. Within the hour a waterborne division of the Metropolitan Police sped over in their launch to investigate us. All three policemen were strikingly large men but professional and cordial. After hearing our story they put us firmly under their patronage. In our tired and anxious state we were only too grateful to have them look after us.

If we imagined that we might now relax for a while, after hardly any sleep in four days, we were sorely mistaken. The water seethed with summer traffic: sightseeing passenger cruisers, official launches, small pleasure craft, even speedboats. With no apparent speed limit, the water is as turbulent as a force five sea, all day long and well into the night. If we were ever going to be seasick it would be here in the Pool of London!

Ken and I raised the main mast ourselves. Help in raising the mizzen came from two of the lads from the boat-yard. They were on their way to a holiday on the River Crouch, but stayed to help from late afternoon until 11pm that night.

The most hazardous operation was to attach the triac cable between the tops of the two masts and the only way it can be done is from the top of the main mast. A quick look up and down the river for a lull in the traffic, then the three of us hauled Ken up as fast as we could, which was a lot faster than he had ever gone up before.

Inevitable! A speedboat whipped out from the far side of the bridge, a three-foot wake attending it. We all shouted a warning 43 feet up to Ken. As *Imago* started to rock wildly the two lads and I clasped waists around the foot of the mast – as if that would do the slightest good – but it showed we cared. I looked up to see Ken in close embrace with the mast top as it whipped him from side to side like a small bird on top of a pine tree in a hurricane. Ken reckons there are teeth marks up there now.

Next day. Tower Bridge Day! The end of all the deadlines. A build-up of tension that made our stomachs churn. Our vessel was ready, bright new flag at the stern, and she looked wonderful.

Chapter 27

Early next morning our friendly policemen arrived to wish us well and to present us with their official plaque: a small mahogany shield depicting two rampant seahorses and a diving beetle. It was a gesture that delighted us. That same morning Ken fixed it to the saloon panelling, where it has remained ever since.

The sails were brought up from below and hanked on. The wind had freshened by late morning but we were determined to motor through with all sails up if we could.

By lunchtime our friends had begun to gather and wave. Always Tower Bridge looming in front of us like a detached paternal presence, we peeled the silver foil from the half bottle of champagne, awaiting our cue...

The clock on the building opposite slowed. At 3.30pm precisely we released the lines and eased out to the middle of the river for the approach – slowly past the museum ship, *The Belfast*. Traffic still moved thick and slow across the bridge. For a moment we wavered. Perhaps it had all been a dream – hold back! Just as *Imago* reached the stern of *The Belfast* the bridge cracked open.

Full throttle ahead. Up with the sails. A slight veer as the wind checked us for a moment then a perfect middle approach as those famous arms rose high in the air.

It really does feel like a personal salute and will always stand out as a moment of moments. All the anxiety and fatigue melted away. We were beating down the Thames through an emotional doorway...

Once we realised that we were passing under at precisely the scheduled time and with dignity, we laughed out loud at each other as we drank the residue of the champagne that had showered the cockpit. Frantic waving from the balustrades and towpath, tourists joining in. No sad departure this, it was pure celebration. We waved back until our arms were numb. *Imago* at last!

Still within sight of Tower Bridge we moored up at a barge where our friends had gathered to greet us. The euphoria lasted for the rest of the day. Fay eventually whisked us off to Romford to be bathed and fed, returning us by midnight – squeaky clean and dozy – to sleep like puppies. At 5am we would begin the journey to the sea. Our plan was to find a berth in Poole, closer to the point where we would eventually set sail for Madeira and the Canary Islands.

The Thames Barrier, shrouded in the pink mist of early morning, gigantic, eerie. Past a skyline bristling with redundant cranes, towards a barren wasteland of rundown industrial sites. As the view widened towards the mouth of the estuary, Ken leaned down to taste the water. Salt! *Imago* was at last in the environment for which she was built.

The 16-hour run to Ramsgate was all pleasure. The beginning of a two-week heatwave. With only the wake from ferries and cargo ships to disturb the sea, we motored all the way – the sky was curved and the expanse of blue and green relaxed us. We didn't bother with watches, just dozed for a few moments when our eyelids refused to open any longer.

By 9pm we were safely berthed in Ramsgate where the harbour personnel received us with great courtesy. For the next few days the tension of the last few weeks was forgotten. We relished the feeling of accomplishment in having travelled by sea to a port of call. Now we must learn to sail.

We left on the morning tide having calculated for a daylight approach into Brighton Marina. A mile out, the wind was light but steady so, for the first time in earnest, we raised the sails.

Quite good on the starboard tack, awful on the port tack. We managed 4.2 knots, just once, but although the average was a bare 2.5 knots, the feel of the boat pulling and the absence of engine noise was a thrilling sensation. We sailed for the next 26 hours, sometimes well, sometimes badly. The sea could not have been more benign towards us, novices that we were.

As darkness closed in we were treated to a wonderfully subtle sunset. Jets had streaked across the sky, criss-crossing the setting sun with pink and violet stripes.

Gradually we began to distinguish the navigation lights of large vessels on the horizon and the dense clusters twinkling out from the resorts along the coastline. A yacht with tan sails loomed too close; in less than a minute she was invisible again. We wondered how she could glide so effortlessly in such a limp wind, but then she was flying a dozen light wind sails and was a classically sleek 60-footer. In these same conditions *Imago*, with her long keel and bulk, tended to wallow – she is a heavy weather vessel.

It was surprisingly chilly through the night hours despite the daytime heatwave. Cold enough for blankets, anoraks, gloves and hot drinks on the hour. Nevertheless this was one of those quiet nights at sea, when it is easier to understand why anyone should take terrible risks just to be here for hours like this, the only sound coming from rustling sails, the rhythmic swish of water against a hull, the underwater sound of your own breathing. Hearing yourself breathe – how unusual that is!

The sea could have taught us a lesson then but chose not to. Hauling in the sails by hand and running the ropes through a trellis-work of pulleys was exhausting. Ken crawled along the decks like a demented crab as we short-tacked along the coast. In any other conditions it would be downright foolhardy. We had two months to get it right but getting it right sounded ominously like money.

We must also establish a proper routine for eating and sleeping on the long hauls. The sea may be a pretty barren landscape but it can mesmerise like a motorway. When the tiredness does come it is both sudden and irresistible. On this first run we took four hours sleep each in one-hour periods.

No doubt it was the excitement that also curbed our appetites. A single slice of bread and a few grape-sized morsels of cheese seemed not only sufficient but also tasted wonderful.

Approaching Brighton, the wind died altogether. Reluctantly, we dropped sail and motored in. It broke the carefree mood, which was just as well since hundreds of boats were rushing in and out of what, after the open sea, looked like an impossibly small entrance. No time for dreaming! We sailed nervously past the long-walled entrance into the marina and were immediately ushered into one of the visiting berths by an attendant – well away from boats made of fibreglass.

The last 24 hours had been a very gentle introduction but we knew well enough that we should not sail again without some modifications. The ropes must lead neatly to the cockpit area or I would undoubtedly lose my skipper – and soon. Also there were more tidying and stowing problems for me to think about.

There is a Parisienne feel about Brighton: an odd mixture of almost cloistered gentility and youthful exuberance. Here in the marina lay vessels from all over Europe, ranging from outfits worth several million pounds, flying personalised crests, to work boats, fishermen and thoroughbred racing yachts. *Imago* occupied a middle-order ranking between the austere and the frivolous. As one brine-encrusted skipper remarked, 'That's a solid looking boat – looks like it's been places.' We thought the best response to that was to smile.

It was decided (by me!) that we should spend £50 of our precious resources on our first genuine holiday in eight years and book in for the week. Amid sounds of labour and leisure, regular food and sleep restored some of our strength though our hair looked rather greyer than only a week before. In reality we were much more tired than either of us realised.

Ken spent his time tinkering with the engine; it had run too hot for his liking, but now he could take his time over it with a hobbyist's pleasure. I busied myself inside and explored the surrounding area.

Brighton is also a truly cosmopolitan city. A dozen languages in as many yards. A newly arrived French boat offered us fresh mackerel even as we took their lines. Ten minutes later we were enjoying a sumptuous lunch with lots of square feet of bread and butter.

At the weekend bikini-clad beauties are draped over every boom and bowsprit. Ken broke two tapping drills while favouring one sultry blonde and wasted the rest of the day looking to replace them.

It was easier to make friends with Lawrence, an engineering sort, who was busy fitting out an old barge. Fiftyish, lively as a spark plug. Within minutes phrases like, 'calibrated chain' and 'Whitworth threads' bounced across the separating pontoons – one of those never to be pursued friendships that stay in the mind.

And so it was that our introduction to the seafaring community began. Inexperience is no bar except from the brash, respect and affection for boats and the sea being the only requirement for membership. Friendships flourish and wane with each tide. Hello and goodbye mean much the same thing. But attitudes are flexible and helpfulness is second nature. Any snobbery that does exist is usually of the inverted sort: the man in the frayed cap with dried fish mucus daubed on his trousers is the man most likely to command respect. White clothes and polished superstructure suggest too comfortable and unchallenging a lifestyle to be envied. No urban posturing or status symbolism worked here. A man was only what he did and could feel as proud of his battered wooden dory as if he were the captain of a clipper ship. Boats, like dogs, are a reflection of their owners, sometimes a happy fact, sometimes not!

Fay and her family joined us for an evening sail. A perfect

windless summer evening so we simply bobbed about outside the harbour walls and ate our supper *al fresco* on deck. The small mackerel caught on the way out were divided between five as hors d'oeuvres, a dessertspoonful each. After walking them back to their car, we strolled back to *Imago* arm in arm, hoping that there would be many more such perfect days. We persuaded them to join us on the third leg to Poole in Dorset. It was there we hoped to find a base and get in some real practice.

When the week was up we left Brighton shortly before midnight with our 'crew'. Fay and I took the dawn watch in zero wind. There followed more experiment with sail configuration than was surely possible with only four to compute. Despite lots of 'belay theres' and giggles, the speed log steadfastly registered 0–0.

By noon on the following day the horizon hazed over and the wind freshened. We recorded our first five knots and 'no land all around'. To avoid the congested Solent we would round the Isle of Wight. As the shadow of the island appeared through the heat haze the sea became choppy and confused. We dropped sail in order to motor into the wind to make up time. Within the next hour waves were approaching from every conceivable direction and doing a fair job of rolling us from scupper to scupper. Conversation petered out. We huddled together in the cockpit.

For the next four and a half hours we tasted the fear. Larger waves at shorter intervals now started to crash over the bowsprit for the first time, scouring the decks, soaking us all to the skin. The mast tops flailed from side to side. Struggling with the wheel to try to meet the worst of it was exhausting but no one offered to relieve me.

Conditions below were impossible. Nothing had been stowed properly in anticipation of heavy weather and although the only casualty was a broken mug, all below was heaped up debris. The spray stung our faces making them red and sore but there was no move to get the wet weather gear from below.

We were well and truly caught out, slap in the middle of the headland current off St Catherine's Point, Isle of Wight.

In deep-sea terms it was not really rough. Not the screaming wind, nil visibility, the mountainous walls of exploding water one reads about. Nor the frozen fatalistic fear that causes sailors' minds to fix in neutral gear. But for all of us, enduring the abrupt change from fair weather to foul for the very first time, and in an untried vessel, was frightening.

Imago danced and rode the sea superbly, a sound test of her structural and rigging strength. Just as we had always felt, only something catastrophic would put her down.

Here endeth both the first lesson and a psychological crash course in humility. It was good for us.

After 46 hours at sea, the ordeal of being caught up in the race, then nearly being run down by a high-speed trawler, we finally made it into Poole Harbour, one of the largest natural harbours in the world – and promptly ran aground! We had veered from the main channel by less than a yard, looking for a mooring. We felt terribly embarrassed until learning later that it was quite par for the course in these shallow silted waters.

The trawler incident saddened us all. It happened during the crossing from the Needles to Poole Bay. In perfect visibility, with no other craft in sight, it steamed across our bows at high speed with less than 15 feet to spare. Clearly the motive was to intimidate a few 'yachties' and in that they were entirely successful.

Later, safely moored alongside the town quay, we all set to, cleaning up the debris, mopping up. After a simple dinner, and long before darkness, we were all firmly asleep.

The cheapest berth lay at the back of the harbour. A pretty berth, especially at night with the lights from the perimeter of the town reflecting from the water on one side and the hundreds of boat masts on the other. Low tide revealed acres of mud flats, long-established feeding grounds for hundreds of wading birds: sandpipers, heron, oyster catchers, the acrobatic gulls and terns.

From here we ventured out most weekends. The winds remained light but we hoped to become adequate sailors through sheer practice. Each time we returned to the mooring we longed to be out again, to be part of that sparkling sea. But we were never tested.

During one memorable sail from Poole to the Needles we saw more than a dozen huge jellyfish swimming side on against the current – creamy coloured monsters as round as dustbin lids with the bulk of a 40-gallon drum, each with its own distinctive tints of subtle blues and pinks. Magnificent creatures and by all accounts completely harmless. We were thrilled. On the same trip we tracked a satellite across the whole of the visible sky and spotted several shooting stars. What we most appreciated was the time to enjoy such sights.

Here, next door to Cowes and the Solent, is the British mecca of yachting. At any time of the week during the summer months there are literally thousands of boats. From a distance they look like so many rows of shark's teeth jutting from the water. Some of the most beautiful and prestigious yachts in the world are assembled here in one vast promenade.

Final preparations. Last inoculations: for typhoid, malaria, cholera, yellow fever. Surely the prospect of fatal diseases posed a more life-threatening danger than the journey itself! The typhoid jab was especially painful. Ken offered his left arm; foolishly, I presented my right. We were then obliged to sit and sleep apart for the next 48 hours.

Ten days before we planned to leave we met Jimmy and Renate, new owners of a very smart wooden motor sailor called *Barbaree*. We took to them instantly, and they to us. Within the week we had become inseparable. Jimmy was as dour and stocky as a Scottish man could be, Renate as determined and organised as any frau. Both enchanted us with their humour. What with Ken's cockney, Jimmy's brogue and Renate's perfect but idiosyncratic English, we had only to talk all at once to be convulsed with friendly laughter.

Barbaree had cost Jimmy most of his savings from gruelling tours with the offshore oil companies. Like us he had never sailed before. His plan was to sail as far as the French and Spanish borders to spend the summer. Within hours of meeting we agreed to travel together until he turned south east and we carried on south to Cape Finisterre, then across to Madeira. It seemed like a sensible arrangement. Ken's navigation was better than Jimmy's while *Barbaree*'s equipment was more sophisticated than ours. Her on-board instrumentation included radar, satellite navigator, wind speed and direction indicator, and even a single-side-band (SSB) radio.

Those last few days were like the build-up to Christmas. Last-minute shopping, every day a new list of things to be done, filling up the food lockers, packaging things. We took dried vegetables and fruit, tins of meat, fish and beans, dried milk, tea, preserves, rice, spaghetti, a sack of potatoes. My sister Brenda contributed a large bag of treats, each item carefully thought about and exactly right.

Suddenly it was only hours. Ahead lay the entirely new challenge of 1,200 miles of ocean; 16 to 21 days of sailing – day and night. We plotted the course to take us towards Plymouth, over to Ushant, across the notorious Bay of Biscay to the Canary Islands.

I reread letters from friends and family then packed them away carefully in a waterproof wallet. They would be even more precious in the future.

Rolled up inside a mug in the cup locker was £70 in cash. We left Cobb's Quay in Poole not owing anyone a penny, neither person, nor bank, except a fortune in gratitude – and it felt like freedom.

Renate and I walked up to the customs office to post the

declaration forms. 'Spain' declared one ... 'Extended voyage' declared the other. After patting them into the box we looked at each other in the way that married women do. Our men were adventurers, dreamers some would say, but each had worked hard to test their dream and make it happen. Whatever anxieties we harboured we would see it through with them ... for better or for worse, as they say...

I just hoped that providence would once again shine on us and preserve us all from harm. That the sea itself might take us was acceptable but what of drug runners, political upheavals, being blown up for target practice, not being allowed to disembark on foreign soil because of some current or historical grievance? As if the sea itself were not enough!

So it was then. The owl and the pussy cat went to sea in a beautiful ... green boat.

Chapter 28

At 6pm precisely, on 30 August 1987, we released our lines from the mooring buoys. This was surely the moment Ken had held fast in his mind for more than eight years – yet something was amiss. The sort of happiness that should have echoed all the other happy times in both our lives wasn't with us. Instead, the atmosphere was tense, anxious, even irritable.

Just below the surface of this muddle of emotions lay the truth. I believe we even looked at it square on, yet still denied it, so impatient were we to begin our journey.

As to what that truth was? It would make its face known soon enough. What is more, it would insist, not once but several times, that we acknowledge it.

Ken was at his worst so I knew he was anxious too. A fresh wind had persisted all day and was now blowing about in spiteful gusts. Three hundred yards in front of us *Barbaree* moved out from her pontoon berth. As we increased throttle to take close order with her the engine coughed for the first time ever – and stopped! *Imago* slewed round as the next gust of wind took her stern, threatening to smash her into the line of moored boats. A frenzied effort with the anchor saved an unthinkable disaster with only inches to spare. Cursing with frustration, Ken bled the engine. Within a few moments we were moving again, only to edge too far from the narrow channel and run aground.

The whole careful strategy of a relaxed and enjoyable meander to Studland Bay, a mile from the harbour entrance, so that we would be in a relaxed frame of mind for the start of our journey, now lay at our feet in an ugly heap.

It was as if Ken had been felled. Something monstrous had

ripped the life out of him. I knew so well the man that raged ... but here with me now was a stranger. His shoulders dropped heavily as if the joints had suddenly dislocated; his head sank slowly onto his chest.

Even as I ran to cast off the dinghy I heard myself crying in sobbing gasps: the weight of his burden was in my own mind and it was too heavy to carry.

'Throw the stern rope! I'll tie it onto the buoy ... you can winch us off,' I shouted to him. Still he stood, an oldness to his shape. I don't believe he even heard me. I would rather have been beaten with burning wood than this. It was unbearable.

I have often wondered since why the emotion that followed should be rage, but it surely was. A violent rage that seemed directed at Ken himself. Perhaps it is the same as those critical moments in combat when soldiers bully their casualties to keep them going. Anyway, I now screamed at him.

'Throw the rope, you bloody idiot!' Still he did not move and the longer he stayed the harder I cried for him.

Finally he exhaled a long shuddering sigh, raised his head slowly and looked across. Now I begged him.

'Come on, skipper!'

At last the rope snaked towards the dinghy. A couple of turns on the winch hauled us round and off. Back on board, we never mentioned any of it. The whole drama had lasted a little under 15 minutes – there was still time to catch the 6.30pm opening of the bridge separating the inner and outer harbours. In silence we motored on briskly. A tail end of yachts was still streaming through and there in the middle of them was *Barbaree* holding back for us.

Passing the town quay, we heard a hail from one of the freight vessels unloading in the dock area. It came again, a northern accent.

'*Imago!*'

A small man sporting both full beard and a lion mane of hair squeezed out from the cockpit of his deck crane, calling out to us again as he ran towards the stern of his ship.

'That's a good-looking boat – have you been far?'

There it was. One of the spoonfuls. Never would there be an all-at-once moment of joy; instead, there would be dozens, no hundreds of them, in small spoonfuls, and no less precious for that. Like this one:

'We are going across the Atlantic,' Ken shouted up at him with a wave... 'Today!' He added.

'You've got the right sort for that – good luck to you.'

With that blessing came the heady feeling that at last we were truly on our way.

Despite the headwind and choppy sea, both craft lay safely anchored in the bay not much more than an hour after setting out. Now we did our best to reassure each other. It wasn't, after all, too remote from what we had planned, never mind this bothersome mixture of excitement and apprehension. This must all be quite normal in situations like this. After years of imagining ... here we are ... the supposed finishing line no different, now that we see it, from another starting point. Every experience from now on would be a beginning and a first.

At about 8pm I saw a flashing light from the beach some 400 yards away. We had planned a last fish and chip supper with friends who lived locally. Guessing it was them, I called over to Ken on *Barbaree*, where he was helping Jimmy with a battery problem.

The wind had settled into a steady force six. Even *Imago* rode quite lively at her anchor. A trip both ways in the dinghy could be risky but the need to see friends on this eve of our departure felt urgent: besides, another disappointment just now would really spoil things.

Ken decided he would paddle over but not attempt to bring them aboard as conditions might get rougher still. I knew he would risk the danger to see them so, beyond urging him to take care and keep flashing a torch, I said nothing to deter him. He had need of this solitary challenge.

The dinghy disappeared quickly into the thick blackness. It felt lonely and forlorn to be on board without Ken. The wind rumbled like a distant locomotive. No stars above. I could just about hear the surf breaking on the sand above the sound of the waves slopping against the hull.

It was uncomfortable below, so for the most part I kept watch from the stern. After two hours my thoughts turned morbid. Surely I couldn't lose my gallant, dearly loved skipper like this? Another half hour ... no, in just a few more minutes I would start up the engine and motor in towards the shore.

As I flashed the torch again, was that an answering light? Not convinced, I flashed again, called out ... and suddenly there he was, caught for a second in the wavering beam of light, arms flailing, wet through, grinning!

Half filled with water, the dinghy careened through the short wave crests inches at a time. Another half hour passed between seeing him and hearing the thump of the dinghy against the hull.

Ken had missed seeing our friends, in spite of the effort. It had taken him nearly an hour of paddling furiously just to make shore. By then they had probably decided for themselves that it was too dangerous for us to come out to them. But it did not seem to matter so much now. One day Ken could tell them how hard he had tried.

Sometime later, the supper things cleared away, we sat together quietly at last, nearing the end of what had been an extraordinarily long and eventful day – each with our separate thoughts – happy to be together.

Ken's tussle in the dinghy acted as a catharsis. Recovering now from such an effort, he could, for a brief time at least, lay aside some of his anxieties. Mine, too, had evaporated the instant he was safely back on board.

Nevertheless, we slept fitfully, dozing off when the movement was rhythmic, snapping awake each time the wake from a ferry or merchant ship smashed along our hull, sending a shudder through the rigging. Every two hours we checked that the anchor held firm.

Next morning all was bustling excitement aboard both vessels with much toing and froing in dinghies. There was still a brisk wind but the sun glinting from the sea transformed the bay from the eerie threatening place of the previous night into a bright and pretty postcard view. We longed to be on our way.

At mid-morning the call rang out at last from *Barbaree*.

'I'm hauling up the anchor.'

With her roller reefing and smart winches, *Barbaree* handled her sails more smoothly than we could, and since she would also be faster than us in most conditions she would lead the way. Both radios crackled...

'You ready then, Ken?'

'Ready, Jimmy. Let's go!'

Chapter 29

With everyone on board in good spirits, the two small ships motored against the wind towards Plymouth, keeping well out from the coast. That first day, the VHF radios were used rather more than is necessary because we so enjoyed hearing Jimmy or Renate cheerfully confirm our bearing. At civilised land hours one of us would go below to brew the tea.

Late that evening we were suddenly enveloped in a swirling mist. It locked out the twilight, leaving a malevolent yellowness through which we slowly groped our way. Long tendrils weaved in and out of the rigging and looking astern we could see our wake carving itself through the substance until the soft streamers joined up again.

The bird flew in from the fog. Tiny, fragile. For a while she sat in the rigging; a faint breeze blew her feathers into curls. It was not the first time this willow warbler had boarded a vessel at sea: she knew exactly what she was about. Starting at the bow, she systematically examined every single shackle and bottle screw, every conceivable fitting that might harbour an insect. She knew precisely where to look, how to place her feet in the rigging to allow for a comfortable examination of each hopeful crevice. Hopping along the deck, inches from us, not once did she flinch or even look our way. When Ken put out his hand, she simply used it as a ramp on her way to the next stanchion.

This same bird had nested somewhere in England, hiding away from even a hint of human presence. Yet here, aboard our boat, indeed on any other boat at sea, she knew, as surely as her forebears must have known, that no harm would come to her. Ken and I looked at each other. If the sea was an environment where respect for other living things is the rule then that was the place for us. Warmed as we were by the behaviour of the warbler, there was, too, an agony of guilt and sadness about it. What is it that we have all done to this earth? And what, on this earth, can we do about it?

Some time after 2am, Ken suggested I try to get some sleep. He would check with Jimmy every half hour for a radar update in case we were too close to merchant shipping. He would tap firmly on the deck twice if he needed me.

Removing only my waterproofs, I lay on top of the bunk listening to the regular creaking of the steering system as Ken held our course. Eventually I must have dozed off...

...the tapping had sounded more than once – had figured in my dreaming. I snapped awake, was on the move, even as I heard it again – this time a hard thump. Either Ken was exasperated or it was a matter of real urgency. The hatch cover was half open. I could see Ken standing at the wheel; everything looked fine. How well I must have slept after all – the mist had cleared and it was nearly light!

'What do you think of that then?' Ken pointed slightly to starboard with a nod of his head. Pushing my body through the opening I swivelled round to look – then gasped in horror!

It was indeed light out there but dawn was still several hours away. Not 30 yards off lay a huge block of flats, every storey festooned with lights; behind it a massive trail of foaming sea.

'Why did you get so damned close?' I accused.

'I was trying to avoid it, love.'

I looked at him very hard. However ridiculous his statement sounded it was transparently clear from the expression on his face that he spoke the truth. Having first spotted it on the horizon he guessed from its size that it was a cross-Channel ferry, but felt it unwise to alter course until he was sure of its direction. Somewhere, hidden amongst a thousand fairy lights, was the crucial port or starboard navigation light.

Ken later surmised that in watching so closely as the huge ship bore down on him he must have turned with it instead of away from it. *Barbaree* had copied every move made by *Imago* and Renate reckoned they did two full circles!

'How close?' I asked.

'Very close.'

My own watch passed uneventfully: not even the masthead light from another yacht, let alone a floating seaside resort.

Ken managed a couple of hours sleep before dawn, not nearly enough, but we both felt fit and enthusiastic, still drinking it all in, on this our second day at sea.

As yet we had not sailed. Our course was still parallel with the coast and the sea remained as placid as an inland waterway in summer. Late in the morning, traces of mist reappeared. By lunchtime it had settled into a dense fog. Only 50 yards ahead *Barbaree* started to go fuzzy at the edges, then disappeared. Immediately we checked our course heading, trusting that Jimmy would do the same. Five minutes later the radio crackled: '*Barbaree, Imago. Barbaree, Imago.*'

Jimmy had slowed, hoping to sight us, but now he was circling. We worried that he might come upon us too quickly to take evasive action.

The next hour was quite comical. Our radar signature showing on Jimmy's radar wasn't precise enough to use in tracking us down. By agreement we both reduced speed and shouted across the water. We heard each other plainly. Surely we were close enough to reach out and touch? But our surroundings remained as blank as ever. Ken stood at the end of the bowsprit pointing at the sound while I helmed. Each time I chugged gently in that direction the voices would come again from a quite different quarter.

We found them at last, over an hour after losing sight of them

– or perhaps they found us. More likely it was entirely accidental as their approach came from port astern while our arms still stretched toward dead ahead!

Since there was little point in repeating such a time-wasting exercise we tied the boats together. Renate and I chatted, leaving Ken and Jimmy to disappear into the bilges of *Barbaree* to see if there was any way of boosting the batteries. It was becoming a problem since without fully charged batteries he would be unable to supply his navigation aids, in particular the radar.

We were highly vulnerable, just bobbing about together on the edge of the shipping lanes. We all listened anxiously for the propeller sounds from large ships. Having so recently discovered how sound is distorted when muffled by fog, we stationed ourselves at the four compass positions, fingers of the starboard watcher ready at the call to start up engines.

Two freighters passed by some 300 yards off: hazy charcoal-coloured shapes against a false horizon. Minutes later Jimmy called out, 'Submarine!' All heads turned in consternation, then back again in greater dismay towards Ken who had taken a mark on a four-masted brigantine!

All turned out to be seagulls, sitting quietly in groups on the water, black on the milky-coloured surface, like so many magnified etchings.

Our eyes ached from peering so long at the sea. After four hours of considerable strain, our bodies, too, felt stiff and weary. We commented on the fact that we had slept for less than three hours between us in the last thirty-six.

At last a wind stirred from the south-west, lifting the fog rapidly from the surface of the sea. As visibility increased to what we guessed might be a mile, we released the ropes holding the boats together and were soon under way again.

We reached the appropriately named 'Start Point', the jutting piece of headland lying just before the curve into Cornwall, from where it is usual to begin the push south-west towards Ushant. On this, the third day, it was heartening to see the flashing lights on the marker buoys coming up exactly in line with our estimated position on the chart. At least our navigation was proving accurate.

Now we could both raise sail and lay a course for the first outward-bound tack. As expected, *Barbaree*, the lighter vessel by exactly half, and with her tailor-made sails, showed a smart turn of speed in the light wind. She was soon lying well ahead. At each change of tack she headed closer to the wind than was necessary, slowing her own pace so that we might keep up. Eventually the land behind looked like nothing more than a cloud on the horizon until a final trough blotted out the coastline of England.

As we headed across the Channel our spirits were high. *Barbaree* firmly believed that by late next morning the French coast would be visible, that moules were on the menu for dinner! Because of Jimmy's problems with battery power we had decided to join him on a stopover in France so that Ken could give him a hand.

Some time in the middle of my 2am to 6am watch we approached the first of the major shipping lanes: a first-time experience that was frankly nerve-racking. It's just not knowing what to expect, I suppose. What do shipping lanes in the English Channel mean to most people?

They spanned the edge of the horizon like a dotted line, mostly freighters and container ships, the occasional tanker. Since Ken's encounter with the ferry, each vessel I saw, however distant, made me long to tap the hull for Ken to be with me. It might not be so worrying if we could monitor their approach together. We had already shared the same awful nightmare – that one of us might come on watch only to find an empty space behind the wheel.

For an age, the ships appeared to own their own surrealistic horizon. They would simply pass in front of me for ever. Closer in, I could begin to make out the red port lights, showing that they were travelling from west to east. In head-swivelling anxiety I tried desperately to remember what Ken had told me as we pored together over the invaluable volume, *Reed's Recognition of*

Lights. Something about the white lights ... all I could bring to mind was that if I saw both port and starboard colours at the same time then we were on a collision course. Since nearly every account we had read about ocean sailing included a near miss, I waited only until the looming black shapes took on the colour of their hulls before tapping on the deck.

In a much calmer frame of mind, we discussed the direction of each ship, agreeing the moment to start up the engine to motor close behind the stern. It had to be timed well enough to gain clear water before the advance of the following ship.

By dawn we reached the second lane, this time running east to west. One of our calculations went wrong. The container ship was less than 200 yards off and aiming for our cockpit before we realised that our current sailing speed would not be enough to get us by. Ken had been sure it was. I was equally convinced it wasn't. It matters not in the end who proves right in these matters, the moment for decision was fast becoming critical. We leaned forward together to press the ignition button. The engine revved up briefly but as we throttled hard it spluttered ... and died!

We gazed in horror at the monstrous carving knife that was about to slice us neatly in two. It was the ship that veered away, just in time. Our sails rattled and slapped as the huge bow wave swung *Imago* off the wind. We raised our arms in dazed acknowledgement.

A meeting was called for. It wasn't just the problem with the engine: our primitive gear made sail changing cruel work for Ken. Without the help of the engine we sometimes had to wait a frustrating 20 minutes for *Imago* to bring her head round – she was proving to be slow and ponderous.

We felt tired, depressed. In the exposed cockpit the nights were damp and cold; the blankets we wrapped around our shoulders soon became saturated and heavy. Without an autopilot there was never a break from the helm. Four hours on and four hours off had sounded feasible but in reality our sleeping periods amounted to barely three hours in twenty-four. I said it for him.

'I think we should go back for now, repairs will be easier in England.'

Ken picked up the microphone of the VHF to call *Barbaree* and I heard him acknowledge at last the truth we had tried so hard to ignore.

'We need more equipment. We are not ready enough, Jimmy. We are going back to England. Good luck, you two!'

Jimmy and Renate said emotional farewells; in such a short time we had become very close. Jimmy was having problems of his own. His batteries were by now almost too low to maintain a light but they would continue on to France. It was nearer than returning to England and they were running low on fuel.

Turning away, we motored in silence for an hour. *Barbaree* was a speck on the horizon. Ken disappeared below. I knew he was crying.

As the sun broke through the grey clouds he looked up at me through the hatch, then leaned forward to touch my hand. As he did so I turned the wheel hard about.

At precisely that moment a school of dolphins appeared from nowhere – an ordinary enough sight to every sailor but a new and splendid enchantment for us. As we watched them disport around us, squeaking in what is surely a language, they seemed to be celebrating our change of heart. In tandem, sometimes in triplicate, they arched from the sea in unison, each curve, each space between them, exactly symmetrical.

A perfection.

Ken was now in the cockpit. As we slowly closed with *Barbaree* again he turned to me.

'Thanks, love. You'll never regret it.'

And indeed, in spite of what was yet to come ... I never did.

Chapter 30

Jimmy and Renate were delighted. We felt warmed by their regard for us. After resuming radio contact, Jimmy just said, 'You're brave, you two.' We could hear Renate in the background laughing, saying over and over in her delightful German accent. 'I knew they would. I told you so, Jimmy!'

Totally unaware that fatigue was now set on its inexorable spiral, we wondered how our spirits could disintegrate then reassert themselves again so quickly. It felt so overwhelming at the time ... but fatigue it was: the factor, above all others, that would lead to our undoing.

The immediate goal for both vessels now was to get safely into a French port for respite.

Night fell. The sea began to pile up as the wind increased to force seven. We could just about discern lights from the south but dared not attempt to navigate inshore in such poor visibility. It started to rain hard. We spent the rest of the night hours lying a-hull, wallowing it out ten miles off shore.

The wind moderated during the dawn hours but by late morning the gale was back with a vengeance. We smashed our way through heavy seas without making significant headway. In order to preserve fuel *Barbaree* was relying totally on sail and now ran into the teeth of it all. On failing batteries Jimmy made his last call to us.

Even now we hear it. His voice sounded dreadful: neither desperate nor resigned – just terribly tired.

'I'm in Hell ... it's gusting nine ... Renate is below, she's crying.'

Our own problems were fast becoming critical. Ken was bleeding the engine every 20 minutes, an almost impossible task with the boat tossing and heaving about. In the earlier gale a halyard worked loose and had ridden to the top of the main mast, leaving us with only one foresail and an unbalanced rig. Now a shackle sheared so we couldn't sail at all. The steering was heavy and unresponsive. Later that evening the engine header tank developed a leak.

Like all novices, we were startled by the sudden change in conditions: one moment coping well in relatively moderate seas some ten miles off the French coast; the next, vainly struggling to round the rocks known as 'Les Triagoz' to reach the safety of the Port de Morlaix. As rain and gloom blotted out the rocks barely four miles off, we knew we must get away from the coast before nightfall. The gale continued to strengthen.

This last effort had cruelly battered us. Stooped with fatigue, we took turns crouching over the wheel as we skidded the waves – neither chance nor hope of rest.

It should have been exhilarating: *Imago* pushing on under tight foresails and reefed main – at her best. Instead it was misery under bare poles. Both stinging rain and screaming wind taunted us. We bowed in surrender and hoped to be pardoned.

Imago now rolled so badly that waves were breaking over the cockpit sides – drenchings by the bathful. We rubbed at salt sores on our faces and were never more close. I think we loved each other then as much as any two people can. We were too tired for talk and anyway the noise around us was too great.

Midway through that dreadful night Ken realised that our ability to cope if we should be called upon to face disaster was being compromised by exhaustion. He began to have doubts about our safety. He therefore made a skipper's decision to use the strength of the gale to run back to England. By now we were truly exhausted – the tiredness became an object, a thing to fight against all the time.

We called *Barbaree*, suggesting they do the same but we couldn't make out his muffled answer.

Thinking back now, those must have been desperate hours. There were thoughts of selling the boat, adopting a more parochial lifestyle. Perhaps we could find a little patch somewhere: rear rabbits, grow cabbages. And hadn't we done enough? Hadn't we built the boat – sailed her?

Yet all of that was simply a way of making the thought of dry land seem real.

I do not recall a single detail of how we got through the shipping lanes that night: all that does come to mind is the noise of the wind.

Ken was showing an instinct for navigation. He calculated the exaggerated leeway caused by the gale. By the middle of the morning on the following day we were back at Start Point. For a further nine interminable hours we battled both wind and tide to make it into Salcombe Harbour. In the near darkness hundreds of coloured lights flashed out from houses, hotels, streets, and boats. Among them, somewhere, the crucial navigation lights that marked out an intricate course into the harbour . . . rocks everywhere.

Several of the grub screws in the shaft part of the steering system chose this, of all times, to work loose. With less than 15 degrees of rudder, the business of constantly correcting the wheel from port to starboard and back again nearly tore my shoulders out. So complete was my concentration that I was not even aware that I was crying from the pain. Zigzagging perilously through the channel, we clumsily located the first available mooring buoy. By then it was 9pm. We promptly collapsed.

We had not washed for six days. We were wet through, cold and hungry – but sleep came first. Stumbling from weakness and the unaccustomed stillness, we rolled into our bunk where we stayed unmoving for the next ten hours.

Some awakenings are perfect. Whether it was the sunlight streaming through a porthole to lie warm on my face, or the 'come, awake' cry of the gulls, I was fully conscious long before opening my eyes. After six days and nights of continuous anxiety this feeling of safety was luxurious. I went on dozing in and out of sleep just to prolong the sensation. Eventually I sat up so that I could see out of the porthole.

What a greeting Salcombe offered! All pretty gardens and water-coloured houses climbing up the cliffs, small hotels tucked discreetly among them. At the water's edge dozens of tiny beaches, each with its own sprinkling of happily playing youngsters. Everything about the place suggested the more genteel holiday pastimes: strolling, harbour watching, a good book, tea and cakes on a high veranda, a whole morning with *The Times*.

Later, after we had washed, we paddled the dinghy over to the courtesy moorings on the town side. On legs still rubbery from our time at sea, progress up the narrow horseshoe streets was slow. Near the top, in the high street, we soon found a cafe in which to make up for sparse rations with an enormous cooked breakfast. Hunger was soon satisfied but our thirst for mugs of tea seemed unquenchable. Such talk as could be managed between forkfuls was non-committal. We knew we were of the same mind anyway – just as soon as the current problems could be solved we would try again.

Suitably revitalised, feeling thoroughly content, we strolled along the high street for a time, admiring the low-key concessions to tourism that still left the town so pretty and unspoiled. We sat on one of the many courtesy benches to enjoy the high view. In the valley of the harbour below, *Imago* lay quietly, looking, we thought, particularly beautiful in this glorious setting. It might have been anywhere in the world.

The tide was out, revealing the treacherous approaches. Spanning most of the harbour entrance was a long ridge of jagged rocks and a sandbar, all of it now showing high and dry. If we had failed to follow the instructions in the almanac down to the last fine detail we would certainly have been shipwrecked. I remembered those very rocks sliding by, inches from our hull; being only slightly blacker than the surrounding darkness had made them appear even more sinister. We shuddered at the memory. This was a difficult harbour to enter even in daylight.

Two elegantly dressed women approached, one of them paused in front of us for a moment to enjoy the view.

'Oh my, what a beautiful boat down there. Come over here, Angela ... just look at that!'

'Yes indeed ... the green one, you mean ... isn't that a picture?'

We introduced ourselves, letting them know how much we appreciated their comments. A most animated conversation followed. They were Canadians visiting England as part of a European tour. When we told them that *Imago* had been eight years in the making they shook our hands with great enthusiasm and proceeded to treat us like celebrities, assuring us over and over again that meeting us was a splendid thing to happen to them on holiday. We both blushed over such an onslaught of praise. Still they continued:

'You actually made that boat down there? On your own, just you two? You really did make it?'

By this time we were squirming, as the English do in the face of such overt enthusiasm. Yet by the time we parted (after photographing us with *Imago* in the background) they had succeeded in restoring our self-confidence and determination ... now that *is* goodwill.

'You'll make it, you know – you'll certainly make it,' they called after us.

Yes, we thought, we probably will, and people like you will be most of the reason why. Thank you! We could have hugged them. For heaven's sake ... we should have done!

Back aboard *Imago*, we set about the tasks that would restore our somewhat battered craft to sailing order. Below was a shambles. Where we had cast off soaking wet clothes they lay as they had fallen in horrible heaps. Liberally sprinkled between them were equally sodden tea leaves, evidence of the number of journeys from cooker to hatch that had been aborted. So common had it become during the gales that we had eventually given up trying. I made a mental note to use tea bags in future.

The sink was piled high with washing-up, the cooker top awash with three kinds of soup – all rather squalid really.

It took two days in all, to retrieve the rope from the top of the mast, replace the shackle, repair the air leak in the fuel line, reset the steering, and clear up the debris. All that time we basked in the sunshine of Salcombe.

Early on the third morning the harbour master arrived to collect another daily mooring fee. The unpredicted stopover together with the breakfast binge had swallowed up almost a third of our precious resources. Still, despite it having been such an unscheduled visit, we would remember this safe harbour with much affection.

'Let go astern!' We are off to try again.

This time the lesson would hurt much more than a hard slap – much more...

Chapter 31

As we headed towards France for the third time, the weather continued fair. Although *Imago* was still sluggish in coming about, with a fresh breeze assisting for most of the day, progress was good. This time the shipping lanes held no fears. Threading a way calmly through them under sail, we felt we had the measure of them now. Predictably, the wind was still from the south-west.

Some 30 miles from the so-elusive Ushant, the sea began to pile up yet again. Remembering how quickly conditions had deteriorated off France, we reefed the main sail. Ken then left me to take a full four-hour watch while he busied himself below. There still appeared to be a few problems to sort out in the engine bay.

Alone at the wheel, I could feel the onset of another severe headache. Surprisingly we were never seasick, perhaps the symptoms are neutralised by fear; instead, and just as debilitating, these pile-driving headaches.

No reserves ... nothing left to draw on. The rest in Salcombe might never have been. Once again we are wet through, tired, dispirited.

Ken emerged from the engine bay a full hour before his watch was due. Instead of giving me his customary hug before taking over, he sat on the floor of the cockpit, his back against the washboards of the companionway, face set grim. I saw a pile of misery bubble to the surface in him. I knew then ... I knew that for the moment, and for the first time, he was beaten.

The constant vibration was gradually breaking up the engine accessories. The header tank had ruptured inside; more seriously, a fractured alternator bracket threatened a significant reduction in our battery charging capability and fuel was running low. Though none of these problems could yet be regarded as critical, they must inevitably get worse. In an emergency, every system must be reliable.

As Ken carefully summarised our predicament, it was obvious that only one conclusion was possible: ahead lay simply more trouble, each hour heading south took us further from the materials with which to put things right. Further speculation was pointless: our hopes for that season were well and truly over.

Once again, then, the truth that had nudged at our elbows since setting out: *Imago* was too basic in terms of equipment. The project, after all, had taken too long, and still needed too much of that wretched stuff, money! Some things just cannot be fabricated, but with only two of us aboard, adequate rest periods were vital and for that to happen the sailing had to be made easier.

Thus denied the goal that had fuelled us for so long (for the present at least), the only urge left was to get safely back to England ... just rest for a while ... rest.

Returning to our on-board routine, Ken set a course north and slightly east, heading directly for Poole Bay. By morning we sighted the English coast.

It looked a bleak area with few landmarks: certainly none that matched with those on the chart. Exactly where we were, or how much easterly drift together with tidal flows had affected our course, we couldn't tell. We must choose to turn east or west, of course, but decision making had become a terrible labour somehow.

My own stamina was already so depleted by exhaustion that during the night I had started to hallucinate: seeing and hearing *Barbaree* and islands in mid-Channel. A strange exotic bird kept me company on the starboard rail, voices of friends taking up all the room in my head.

Closer in, still trying to identify a light or landmark. *Imago* skirted a long strip of land. We decided it could only be the Isle of Wight and headed in. Meanwhile, a band of mist and rain, driven by a steadily increasing wind, closed over the land.

Closer still, a lighthouse. While it was the confirmation we needed, it was decidedly not the landfall we would have chosen: the spur of land was Portland Bill. By now a gale force wind had set hard behind us, so that despite strenuous efforts to run back out to sea, an ordeal through those infamous overfalls became inevitable.

What followed proved to be the longest and most violent hours of our entire lives. From the lighthouse it must have looked like a suicide bid – a bare-poled yacht lining up, as if to deliberately ride the falls through the very middle, all the way, one end to the other ... which is exactly what we did.

Imago plunged into this boiling vat of seaway, shaking the water from her decks like a labrador. As vicious curling waves smashed in from every quarter, Ken gently prised my hands from the wheel. This one was for *Imago* and her skipper.

During the first few moments we both feared a capsize. So short and steep were the waves that most proved unavoidable, but Ken had to watch for those that doubled up. A finishing thrust from one of these, if it caught us on the roll, might well put us over.

Ken's eyes were alight! As *Imago* rode and danced amid the noise of the smashing spray, he grinned and shouted. Never more intimately connected to the craft he had built.

It was too late for me to discover the elation of battle fever. I was far too exhausted to understand or care. Sometimes we were poised in the air, higher than the lighthouse – each time my limbs jerked involuntarily.

It was dark before we finally escaped. Now we found ourselves driven very fast along the coast. The speed log failed (brand new, saved for, out of a packet), making it difficult to estimate just when we might turn against the wind, raise some sail, to make Poole Harbour by dawn.

Down below I pored over the chart. If we really were pushing on as fast as I thought, then the safety of the bay lay only four hours away – some time between 2am and 3am. Knowing when it might be mattered in a way that was out of all proportion – it became the difference between hanging on and letting go. Soon we could sleep ... at 0300 at the very latest. Sleep. I watched the chronometer as if it were the Doomsday countdown.

From Portland I was physically incapable of controlling the wheel. We would discover later why that should be, since it had never demanded great strength before. At the time, I could only presume that my body had reached its limits – not an ounce more in you, girl!

Ken, too, was running on mental reserves: the last of his physical energy had been expended in the battle off Portland. I could see him through the hatch cover – both hands clamped to the wheel. Occasionally he licked the salt from his sore lips. His eyes were red and hollow with fatigue.

A series of red lights would confirm our position. Each time Ken called I went out with the binoculars, but poor visibility and big seas made spotting inconclusive. None of the sightings lasted long enough to count or time the flashes. At about the time we had calculated for the turn, two freighters veered away to port. Our running speed was so great that we had kept station with them for many miles. But Ken refused to follow them. His determination to spot the red lights had turned into an obsession – surely another symptom of a terrible weariness.

As 0500 came up, I sat against the hatch, stiff with anxiety. As this last hope of respite dissolved with the passing hours, I had nothing left with which to fight the urge to sleep. My eyes closed ... in my mind I still resisted ... but my eyes had closed.

Chapter 32

Even as the sound of Ken tapping on the hull prised me from sleep, I was aware of a change in the motion of the boat – she was pitching deeply fore and aft.

In the semi-darkness the view from the cockpit was all of one colour: grey water, long grey shapes of land, grey sky. Everything in dismal harmony with the relentless howling wind. For a brief moment the dense mist thinned away to reveal our predicament. We were trapped in a bay with potential disaster on three sides. In front, the only safe area out to sea, our escape, was blocked by what had now become a severe gale against which we could not make a single metre. Huge volumes of water rushed in towards us.

The bleak facts of the situation struck home with a thud of dismay: this was trouble and neither of us were fit enough to handle the situation should it become a matter of survival.

Ken was fighting the wheel just to hold station. He looked ill now. Eyes totally bloodshot, shivering uncontrollably. He had battled alone for ten hours. Even as long ago as the ordeal off Portland we had been relying on gut instincts. These were surely the last milligrams of effort.

At the very least we must find out exactly where we were, there might be an escape route behind us, though we felt pretty certain that we were lying close in to a lee shore somewhere off the Isle of Wight; we had run too far east.

Dawn made little difference to the colour of the day but at least we could now make out an oscillating light off to starboard. The seas were getting even bigger. We could not go on in this dreadful limbo not knowing if the nightmare would end before the day was out.

*　*　*

I called up on the emergency frequency: 'Pan-Pan. Pan-Pan. Pan-Pan.' Any vessel in the vicinity would hear that call and give it their immediate attention; perhaps they could give us a fix on our position.

'Solent coastguard, *Imago*. Solent coastguard, *Imago*.'

For a moment I felt shock at hearing a strange sound, then a surge of relief as I heard it once more, a calm reassuring voice.

I described as best I could the characteristics of the light and the need to verify our position. There was no hesitation. 'You are lying in Freshwater Bay just off the Needles Lighthouse ... madam,' he added, making me feel like a wayward car driver! I thanked him for the position then explained that after a rather rough passage from Portland we were low on fuel and somewhat tired. (What a quaint little understatement that was!)

Since the updated weather forecast warned that conditions were likely to deteriorate even further we were then advised to try and round the Needles into the relatively calmer waters of the Solent. The coastguard would stand by on the emergency frequency so that I could report back on our progress.

As I replaced the receiver, I realised that throughout this exchange tears had streamed down my face although my voice had remained level and unemotional.

We tried, full throttle, to follow the coastguard's advice. The engine itself obliged but the exhaust hose decided just then that it, too, had given its all. As it ruptured, a small fire started in the engine bay. Dense black fumes billowed up into the cockpit. Ken handed over the wheel before catapulting below. Fortunately a single squirt with the CO_2 cylinder was sufficient to put it out.

At the wheel, I tried desperately to keep us heading the waves, but *Imago* did two complete turns, almost lying on her sides as she was lifted broadside. With Ken back from his firefighting detail, I called the coastguard again to report our new predicament. But whoever was on duty in the lighthouse that day had seen the signs of a fire coupled with what looked like a vessel out of control – the Yarmouth lifeboat was already on its way.

Twenty minutes later we spotted the lifeboat as it rounded the point, looking no larger, at that distance, than a small orange buoy, as it crested between the big waves. Skilfully manoeuvring his vessel behind our stern, the coxswain raised a shout – the signal for a man to leap on board. Making his way to the cockpit he looked intently into our faces for a moment.

'You'd better get below, you two, change into some dry clothes and put your lifebelts on – it's going to be rough round that point. I'm in charge here now.'

I don't know what he saw in our eyes, but as he said to us sometime later, in the past it had been in his own eyes. Anyway, he took control, which was just what we needed. Within minutes a tow rope was around our Samson post. The lifeboat nudged ahead to take up the strain.

None of the men acknowledged our presence after that: indeed they seemed to deliberately avoid eye contact. Theirs is the ultimate in teamwork; the only focus for them was the task in hand. Special men.

We watched from below. Our man aboard was undoubtedly a relative of Neptune himself – stockily built, luxuriantly bewhiskered. How the mind fixes on irrelevant detail in times of stress. I was drawn to his feet: he wore no socks and there were more holes than canvas to his deck shoes. It is difficult to guess the age of a seafaring man – he might have been 35 or 55; his hands and cheeks were mahogany brown. He had certainly 'weathered a few' as he put it.

'And we'll have no nonsense from you, my girl,' he said, as he settled himself four square behind the wheel, taking a rein on *Imago* as though she were a recalcitrant mare.

Even with the lifeboat's 1,000 horsepower engine it still took one and a half hours to battle round the point. There was praise for the seaworthiness of *Imago* from Neptune himself. He had expected a thorough wetting and was genuinely impressed that she only shipped one of the waves.

Safely past the Needles, heading for Yarmouth Harbour, we were asked whether we thought the engine would cope with taking us in under our own power. The question puzzled us. The lifeboatman noticed our confusion and grinned broadly.

'We could always release the tow rope just before the entrance. A lot of yachtsmen feel embarrassed about being brought in.'

Embarrassed? After being helped? We felt not the least bit embarrassed, and said so.

'Right ... in we go then.'

Willing hands reached out from the harbour wall to take our lines; heads peered out from the hatch covers of moored yachts. It was only then that we realised that the radio messages had blared out from every marine set in the harbour. A man called down to us.

'You'll be all right now – you sounded very calm out there.'

The lifeboat returned to its station a few yards away. Neptune nodded a farewell. Gradually the heads bobbed down. That was the moment we could believe, truly, that we were safe.

So ended ten days criss-crossing the English Channel without even the satisfaction of a foreign port of call. Some very serious thinking to be done – but not just now.

For the next 24 hours we were left entirely undisturbed. There is a 'knowingness' amongst this small community about the effects of hardship at sea, plenty of folk on that windswept island who knew exactly how we were feeling just then, who knew, too, that the best way to handle it was to leave us to bide our time.

The first thing to savour was the prospect of sleep. First wash the encrusted salt from faces and bodies, brew a decent cup of tea, enjoy an unhurried roll-up cigarette, that for once would stay dry to the end.

After sleeping fitfully for about six hours, we ate a chicken supper at the nearest pub, though it was more a matter of feeling that we should try to eat something than of hunger; yet no amount of fluid could quench our thirsts or bring any moisture back to our mouths. Tea, fruit juice, water, sucking on ice – we tried everything; still, our throats were dry as a desert, and just as full of sand. We spoke little, in gruff whispers.

Shortly before we left, some local fishermen came in. They gathered together around the bar.

'Lifeboat was out early this morning.'

'Two it was – been out in all them gales, they had.'

'Boat's been out twice more since then – be out again, too, if this goes on.'

We would rather not have heard the details, but it was impossible not to overhear some of it. The bar noise had quieted for them: such stories, of storm and rescue, figured large in the history of this community.

On the second call out, two people had been plucked from the water after their boat capsized. On the third, a life raft was brought in from mid-Channel. Inside the raft were two bodies. Only a post-mortem would establish how long those unfortunate souls had spent adrift.

From the description they gave, we knew they were not Jimmy and Renate yet we still did not know how they had fared despite calling the coastguard stations along the southern coast of Britain to see if they had reported in. We fervently hoped and prayed that they, too, were at that moment recovering in a French port.*

Later, still in a state of shock, we sat on the harbour wall to roll a last cigarette before turning in. The tide was out. *Imago*, lying below us, looked peaceful and remarkably unscathed, except for the remnants of her stern flag, barely a half of it left, ragged edges still flailing wildly.

A profound sadness came over us. Our craft had been magnificent. We owed our lives to her robustness. It was we who had let her

---

* We learned, months later, that *Barbaree* had made it safely into Morlaix harbour.

down. Her seaworthiness was beyond doubt: Ken had built a genuine long-distance mariner; what she now deserved was a better history. Beyond that, neither of us had a thought for the future ... first we must get well.

This time, recovery was slow. It was three nights before the saloon stopped waltzing and swaying, before nightmares gave way to restless sleep. Another ten before all the symptoms of dehydration and exposure left us. As well as feeling drained and weak, we looked haggard. Ken had lost nearly two stones in weight and I had lost a stone.

We met several interesting people in Yarmouth: among them was John Corelli. John put us right about many things and was well qualified to offer such advice. Still an active skipper, despite his 70 years, he spent most of his weekends sailing alone on his current boat – a 32-footer. His inexhaustible store of yarns, no doubt honed by many tellings, kept us enthralled. He had once stayed at the helm of an elderly freighter for three days and nights during terrible storms. His small crew remained below. All had succumbed and were nearly suicidal from seasickness.

'I felt like you do now,' said John. 'You must not think that you are over it yet, you know. It will take weeks.'

He seemed to read the trouble in our minds too.

'After each ordeal comes the vow. Never again will you volunteer for such terrible fear and discomfort. Then comes the next time...'

We owe a huge debt to Mr Corelli. No one else could have relieved Ken of his burden of doubt except a man who had sailed all his life, in most types of vessel, with and without the aids of modern technology, in high water and in calm.

'You did remarkably well to get her back safely, you know.'

And the pain in Ken's eyes melted away. If he had been impetuous then it must be balanced, not only against long years of dogged patience, but also against the invaluable lessons that were learned.

John Corelli loved *Imago*! It was as simple as that. Fifty years earlier he might have carved his name with hers into the bark of a tree.

'If you had made me an offer when we were brought in, I might have struck your hand on it,' said Ken ruefully.

John would certainly have bought *Imago* if we had pressed him; he said so. He was equally sure that had he done so she would never be his. He ran his hands along a length of oak. 'You've built your souls into this.' Such understanding brought a lump to our throats.

It was John, too, who was able to account for *Imago*'s sluggishness through the water. He was horrified by the amount of weed and barnacle growth below the water-line.

'Get that off now!' he ordered. 'You have reduced your hull speed and engine rating by something close to sixty per cent.'

He was right of course. Despite cleaning the hull meticulously before we left, the warm shallow waters of Poole Harbour was the optimum environment for marine growth. In less than two months some of the weed had grown several inches long and the barnacles half an inch across. Burdened by the extra weight and such an enormous drag factor, it was small wonder we had staggered about more than we had made headway.

With John's help we scraped and brushed the hull between two tides. The five hour crossing to Poole would show us the effect on her performance.

'Give it time.' That was all John said as he bade us farewell. He took himself off to the top of the cliffs and watched through his binoculars as we motored towards the Needles before raising sail for Poole.

Imago was a different boat. As the foresails filled she ducked her head round, smart as a spaniel. We could feel the lift and surge through the hull as we set off.

Three and a half hours later, without once going below

five knots we were closing with the chain ferry at the harbour entrance.

'Keep her going!' shouted Ken. 'Take her all the way in!

So we did. Winding through the dog-leg channels right up to Town Quay with everything still up. Admiring glances. We were thrilled. For the first time we had done our craft justice, proved beyond any past or future doubt, that none the problems belonged to her.

Epilogue

Was it foolhardy? Will seasoned sailors log this account as another example of inexperienced folk sailing away and coming unstuck?

I can only say that it did not feel like that. There was nothing about the experience, grim though it was, that disqualified us from trying again. The most important questions had been answered: would the vessel do, would her crew do, could we trust each other?

The fear would dwell in us again, very many times, but it was still what we wanted to do – the human spirit is slow to be disillusioned, reluctant to lose faith.

Another year of planning and consolidating, though irksome, now felt worthwhile. Next time we would set out confidently, knowing exactly what equipment would preserve us from the fatigue that was our undoing.

If it was about heeding a lesson then we had listened, we had learned. Just a difference in interpretation really: as the start of a circumnavigation it had been a spectacular failure, but as sea trials it could not have been bettered!

By and large, it was a punishing way to realise that determination should not rule over common sense, especially where elemental forces are concerned. At the same time, it can hardly be termed an 'adventure' if entirely free of risk or hardship.

And there was something out there – more than the fear and the noise – something that would make us try again a dozen times: we were acutely alive, overwhelmingly free.

Boats are a wonderfully rounded symbol of freedom, the kind

that is entered into rather than fought for; that is essentially within us all, waiting to be re-encountered or invited in once more.

A year has passed. We have a smart new dog house, satellite navigator, storm sails in the locker, a self-steering system, a clean anti-fouled hull. The weather is fair and it is almost ten years since Ken laid the keel. In a strange way, the future matters less to me. It was the building of the boat that I found so compelling. To have been involved in every aspect of her construction has been a lifetime privilege. I knew that I had witnessed a great labour – had truly seen a man at work.

As for me? I could never have imagined that the song would be so round and full. It was as if my early life was a rehearsal – a preparation – and that somehow, without its impact, I might never have found the will to dream – my walnut craft might never have reached the sea.

Have we left you wondering?
Did they make it?

POSTSCRIPT

It all happened 15 years and 40,000 miles ago. Ken succeeded in sailing his boat around the globe. Taking the helm of any boat is a fresh encounter with what Dylan Thomas called those 'lamb white days'. Taking the helm of a boat you have built yourself is the precious adult version. And was it worth the effort? Did the end justify the means? It did for us, which is all we will say, because it would be wrong to imagine it will be the same for anyone else. But sailing the oceans remains a singular experience and it can never be less than a huge adventure.

* * *

Raroia, the island in the Tuamotus where *Kon Tiki* finally fetched up on the outer reef. Mid-Pacific, a seven-mile-wide horseshoe reef, a Technicolor Disneyland of fish and coral. As the tide turned, a flotilla of juvenile manta rays passed through the anchorage. Their 'wings' were barely eight feet wide. At maturity they would cast a shadow 22 feet wide. One by one they passed by, undulating, in a perfect ballet, as liquid as the water they inhabited. We watched them until our eyes ached, can never forget them. Just one experience. We might have been the only ones to see it. And for that one moment everything we had done was made worthwhile.

We continue to believe that all dreams are special, and should be preserved, which is to say that they must always seem possible whatever the odds. Perhaps they are even more important just now. There is evidence that we have been seduced into a pace of living, a value system, and an artificial environment that does not suit the human spirit.

Ken made a dream come true for what are known as ordinary people. I'm not sure that anything quite like it has been seen before.

This is my tribute to him.

Acknowledgements

Philip and Elizabeth Smith were parents every child should be blessed with. Adopting a hurt child is always a brave and caring gesture, especially so when undertaken in middle age when your own children are adults. Although both they and Peggy are now dead, I have my dear sister Brenda to remember them by. Also my niece and nephew Jane and Philip, each of whom I love and admire. There is a Philip and Elizabeth in all of them: Jane is a paediatric nurse, Philip and his partner Sue are foster parents. Jane is mother of great nephews Luke and Jamie. Although Jamie was taken from us by that wretched disease cystic fibrosis, he remains present. I cannot recall anything in my own life that could hurt us all so much. It may sound strange, even morbid, to declare that you are ready for death (not wanting to die of course, but in the sense that you are already at peace); that to expect anything more of such a splendid life would be just plain greedy!

Family and friends ... without them there could not have been a Dragonfly Imago, neither literally nor metaphorically. Ken and I are grateful for this opportunity to acknowledge you all.

Finally, the text on pages 209–215 of this book is based on an article I wrote for *Practical Boat Owner*, which was published in that magazine in October 1991, issue 298.